STAR BORN

ANDRE NORTON

Star Born

Andre Norton

© 1st World Library, 2007
PO Box 2211
Fairfield, IA 52556
www.1stworldlibrary.com
First Edition

LCCN: 2007930713

Softcover ISBN: 978-1-4218-4790-0
Hardcover ISBN: 978-1-4218-4693-4
eBook ISBN: 978-1-4218-4887-7

Purchase *"Star Born"*
as a traditional bound book at:
www.1stWorldLibrary.com/purchase.asp?ISBN=978-1-4218-4790-0

1st World Library is a literary, educational organization
dedicated to:

- Creating a free internet library of downloadable ebooks

- Hosting writing competitions and offering book publishing
  scholarships.

Interested in more 1st World Library books? contact:
literacy@1stworldlibrary.com
Check us out at: www.1stworldlibrary.com

1ˢᵗ World Library Literary Society

Giving Back to the World

"If you want to work on the core problem, it's early school literacy."

- James Barksdale, former CEO of Netscape

"No skill is more crucial to the future of a child, or to a democratic and prosperous society, than literacy."

- Los Angeles Times

"Literacy... means far more than learning how to read and write... The aim is to transmit... knowledge and promote social participation."

- UNESCO

"Literacy is not a luxury, it is a right and a responsibility. If our world is to meet the challenges of the twenty-first century we must harness the energy and creativity of all our citizens."

- President Bill Clinton

"Parents should be encouraged to read to their children, and teachers should be equipped with all available techniques for teaching literacy, so the varying needs and capacities of individual kids can be taken into account."

- Hugh Mackay

"What of our children--the second and third generations born on this new world? They will have no memories of Terra's green hills and blue seas. Will they be Terrans—or something else?"

—TAS KORDOV, *Record of the First Years*

1

SHOOTING STAR

The travelers had sighted the cove from the sea—a narrow bite into the land, the first break in the cliff wall which protected the interior of this continent from the pounding of the ocean. And, although it was still but midafternoon, Dalgard pointed the outrigger into the promised shelter, the dip of his steering paddle swinging in harmony with that wielded by Sssuri in the bow of their narrow, wave-riding craft.

The two voyagers were neither of the same race nor of the same species, yet they worked together without words, as if they had established some bond which gave them a rapport transcending the need for speech.

Dalgard Nordis was a son of the Colony; his kind had not originated on this planet. He was not as tall nor as heavily built as those Terran outlaw ancestors who had fled political enemies across the Galaxy to establish a foothold on Astra, and there were other subtle differences between his generation and the parent stock.

Thin and wiry, his skin was brown from the gentle toasting of the summer sun, making the fairness of his closely cropped hair even more noticeable. At his side was his long bow, carefully wrapped in water-resistant flying-dragon skin, and from the belt which supported his short breeches of tanned duocorn hide swung a two-foot blade—half wood-knife, half sword. To the eyes of his Terran forefathers he would have presented a barbaric picture. In his own mind he was amply clad and armed for the man-journey which was both his duty and his heritage to make before he took his place as a full adult in the Council of Free Men.

In contrast to Dalgard's smooth skin, Sssuri was covered with a fluffy pelt of rainbow-tipped gray fur. In place of the human's steel blade, he wore one of bone, barbed and ugly, as menacing as the spear now resting in the bottom of the outrigger. And his round eyes watched the sea with the familiarity of one whose natural home was beneath those same waters.

The mouth of the cove was narrow, but after they negotiated it they found themselves in a pocket of bay, sheltered and calm, into which trickled a lazy stream. The gray-blue of the seashore sand was only a fringe beyond which was turf and green stuff. Sssuri's nostril flaps expanded as he tested the warm breeze, and Dalgard was busy cataloguing scents as they dragged their craft ashore. They could not have found a more perfect place for a camp site.

Once the canoe was safely beached, Sssuri picked up his spear and, without a word or backward glance, waded out into the sea, disappearing into the depths, while his companion set about his share of camp tasks. It was still early in the summer—too early to expect to find ripe fruit. But Dalgard rummaged in his voyager's bag and brought out a half-dozen crystal beads. He laid these out on a flat-topped stone by the stream, seating himself cross-legged beside it.

To the onlooker it would appear that the traveler was meditating. A wide-winged living splotch of color fanned by overhead; there was a distant yap of sound. Dalgard neither looked nor listened. But perhaps a minute later what he awaited arrived. A hopper, its red-brown fur sleek and gleaming in the sun, its eternal curiosity drawing it, peered cautiously from the bushes. Dalgard made mind touch. The hoppers did not really think—at least not on the levels where communication was possible for the colonists—but sensations of friendship and good will could be broadcast, primitive ideas exchanged.

The small animal, its humanlike front pawhands dangling over its creamy vest, came out fully into the open, black eyes flicking from the motionless Dalgard to the bright beads on the rock. But when one of those paws shot out to snatch the treasure, the traveler's hand was already cupped protectingly over the hoard. Dalgard formed a mental picture and beamed it at the twenty-inch creature before him. The hopper's ears twitched nervously, its blunt nose wrinkled, and then it bounded back into the brush, a weaving line of moving grass marking its retreat.

Dalgard withdrew his hand from the beads. Through the years the Astran colonists had come to recognize the virtues of patience. Perhaps the mutation had begun before they left their native world. Or perhaps the change in temperament and nature had occurred in the minds and bodies of that determined handful of refugees as they rested in the frozen cold sleep while their ship bore them through the wide, uncharted reaches of deep space for centuries of Terran time. How long that sleep had lasted the survivors had never known. But those who had awakened on Astra were different.

And their sons and daughters, and the sons and daughters of

two more generations were warmed by a new sun, nourished by food grown in alien soil, taught the mind contact by the amphibian mermen with whom the space voyagers had made an early friendship—each succeeding child more attuned to the new home, less tied to the far-off world he had never seen or would see. The colonists were not of the same breed as their fathers, their grandfathers, or great-grandfathers. So, with other gifts, they had also a vast, time-consuming patience, which could be a weapon or a tool, as they pleased—not forgetting the instantaneous call to action which was their older heritage.

The hopper returned. On the rock beside the shining things it coveted, it dropped dried and shriveled fruit. Dalgard's fingers separated two of the gleaming marbles, rolled them toward the animal, who scooped them up with a chirp of delight. But it did not leave. Instead it peered intently at the rest of the beads. Hoppers had their own form of intelligence, though it might not compare with that of humans. And this one was enterprising. In the end it delivered three more loads of fruit from its burrow and took away all the beads, both parties well pleased with their bargains.

Sssuri splashed out of the sea with as little ado as he had entered. On the end of his spear twisted a fish. His fur, slicked flat to his strongly muscled body, began to dry in the air and fluff out while the sun awoke prismatic lights on the scales which covered his hands and feet. He dispatched the fish and cleaned it neatly, tossing the offal back into the water, where some shadowy things arose to tear at the unusual bounty.

"This is not hunting ground." His message formed in Dalgard's mind. "That finned one had no fear of me."

"We were right then in heading north; this is new land." Dalgard got to his feet.

On either side, the cliffs, with their alternate bands of red, blue, yellow, and white strata, walled in this pocket. They would make far better time keeping to the sea lanes, where it was not necessary to climb. And it was Dalgard's cherished plan to add more than just an inch or two to the explorers' map in the Council Hall.

Each of the colony males was expected to make his man-journey of discovery sometimes between his eighteenth and twentieth year. He went alone or, if he formed an attachment with one of the mermen near his own age, accompanied only by his knife brother. And from knowledge so gained the still-small group of exiles added to and expanded their information about their new home.

Caution was drilled into them. For they were not the first masters of Astra, nor were they the masters now. There were the ruins left by Those Others, the race who had populated this planet until their own wars had completed their downfall. And the mermen, with their traditions of slavery and dark beginnings in the experimental pens of the older race, continued to insist that across the sea—on the unknown western continent—Those Others still held onto the remnants of a degenerate civilization. Thus the explorers from Homeport went out by ones and twos and used the fauna of the land as a means of gathering information.

Hoppers could remember yesterday only dimly, and instinct took care of tomorrow. But what happened today sped from hopper to hopper and could warn by mind touch both merman and human. If one of the dread snake-devils of the interior was on the hunting trail, the hoppers sped the warning. Their vast curiosity brought them to the fringe of any disturbance, and they passed the reason for it along. Dalgard knew there were a thousand eyes at his service whenever he wanted them. There was little chance of being taken by surprise, no matter how dangerous this journey north might be.

"The city—" He formed the words in his mind even as he spoke them aloud. "How far are we from it?"

The merman hunched his slim shoulders in the shrug of his race. "Three days' travel, maybe five. And it"—though his furred face displayed no readable emotion, the sensation of distaste was plain—"was one of the accursed ones. To such we have not returned since the days of falling fire—"

Dalgard was well acquainted with the ruins which lay not many miles from Homeport. And he knew that that sprawling, devastated metropolis was not taboo to the merman. But this other mysterious settlement he had recently heard of was still shunned by the sea people. Only Sssuri and a few others of youthful years would consider a journey to explore the long-forbidden section their traditions labeled as dangerous land.

The belief that he was about to venture into questionable territory had made Dalgard evasive when he reported his plans to the Elders three days earlier. But since such trips were, by tradition, always thrusts into the unknown, they had not questioned him too much. All in all, Dalgard thought, watching Sssuri flake the firm pink flesh from the fish, he might deem himself lucky and this quest ordained. He went off to hack out armloads of grass and fashion the sleep mats for the sun-warmed ground.

They had eaten and were lounging in content on the soft sand just beyond the curl of the waves when Sssuri lifted his head from his folded arms as if he listened. Like all those of his species, his vestigial ears were hidden deep in his fur and no longer served any real purpose; the mind touch served him in their stead. Dalgard caught his thought, though what had aroused his companion was too rare a thread to trouble his less acute senses.

"Runners in the dark—"

Dalgard frowned. "It is still sun time. What disturbs them?"

To the eye Sssuri was still listening to that which his friend could not hear.

"They come from afar. They are on the move to find new hunting grounds."

Dalgard sat up. To each and every scout from Homeport the unusual was a warning, a signal to alert mind and body. The runners in the night—that furred monkey race of hunters who combed the moonless dark of Astra when most of the higher fauna were asleep—were very distantly related to Sssuri's species, though the gap between them was that between highly civilized man and the jungle ape. The runners were harmless and shy, but they were noted also for clinging stubbornly to one particular district generation after generation. To find such a clan on the move into new territory was to be fronted with a puzzle it might be well to investigate.

"A snake-devil—" he suggested tentatively, forming a mind picture of the vicious reptilian danger which the colonists tried to kill on sight whenever and wherever encountered. His hand went to the knife at his belt. One met with weapons only that hissing hatred motivated by a brainless ferocity which did not know fear.

But Sssuri did not accept that explanation. He was sitting up, facing inland where the thread of valley met the cliff wall. And seeing his absorption, Dalgard asked no distracting questions.

"No, no snake-devil—" after long moments came the answer. He got to his feet, shuffling through the sand in the curious little half dance which betrayed his agitation more strongly than his thoughts had done.

"The hoppers have no news," Dalgard said.

Sssuri gestured impatiently with one outflung hand. "Do the hoppers wander far from their own nest mounds? Somewhere there—" he pointed to the left and north, "there is trouble, bad trouble. Tonight we shall speak with the runners and discover what it may be."

Dalgard glanced about the camp with regret. But he made no protest as he reached for his bow and stripped off its protective casing. With the quiver of heavy-duty arrows slung across his shoulder he was ready to go, following Sssuri inland.

The easy valley path ended less than a quarter of a mile from the sea, and they were fronted by a wall of rock with no other option than to climb. But the westering sun made plain every possible hand and foot hold on its surface.

When they stood at last on the heights and looked ahead, it was across a broken stretch of bare rock with the green of vegetation beckoning from at least a mile beyond. Sssuri hesitated for only a moment or two, his round, almost featureless head turning slowly, until he fixed on a northeasterly course—striking out unerringly as if he could already sight the goal. Dalgard fell in behind, looking over the country with a wary eye. This was just the type of land to harbor flying dragons. And while those pests were small, their lightning-swift attack from above made them foes not to be disregarded. But all the flying things he saw were two moth birds of delicate hues engaging far over the sun-baked rock in one of their graceful winged dances.

They crossed the heights and came to the inland slope, a drop toward the central interior plains of the continent. As they plowed through the high grasses Dalgard knew they were under observation. Hoppers watched them. And once through a break in a line of trees he saw a small herd of duocorns race into the shelter of a wood. The presence of those two-horned creatures, so like the pictures he had seen of Terran horses, was insurance that the snake-devils did not hunt in this district, for the swift-footed duocorns were never found within a day's journey of their archenemies.

Late afternoon faded into the long summer twilight and still Sssuri kept on. As yet they had come across no traces of Those Others. Here were none of the domed farm buildings, the monorail tracks, the other relics one could find about Homeport. This wide-open land could have been always a wilderness, left to the animals of Astra for their own. Dalgard speculated upon that, his busy imagination supplying various reasons for such tract. Then the voiceless communication of his companion provided an explanation.

"This was barrier land."

"What?"

Sssuri turned his head. His round eyes which blinked so seldom stared into Dalgard's as if by the intensity of that gaze he could drive home deeper his point.

"What lies to the north was protected in the days before the falling fire. Even *Those*"—the distorted mermen symbol for Those Others was sharpened by the very hatred of all Sssuri's kind, which had not paled during the generations since their escape from slavery to Astra's one-time masters—"could not venture into some of their own private places without special leave. It is perhaps true that the city we are seeking is one of those restricted ones and that this wilderness is a boundary for it."

Dalgard's pace slowed. To venture into a section of land which had been used as a barrier to protect some secret of Those Others was a highly risky affair. The first expedition sent out from Homeport after the landing of the Terran refugee ship had been shot down by robot-controlled guns still set against some long-dead invader. Would this territory be so guarded? If so they had better go carefully now—

Sssuri suddenly struck off at an angle, heading not northeast now, but directly north. The brush lands along the foot of the cliffs gave way to open fields, bare except for the grass rippled by the wind. It was not the type of country to attract the night runners, and Dalgard wondered a little. They should discover water, preferably a shallow stream, if they wanted to find what the monkey creatures liked best.

Within a quarter-hour he knew that Sssuri was not going wrong. Cradled in a sudden dip in the land was the stream Dalgard had been looking for. A hopper lifted a dripping muzzle from the shore ripples and stared at them. Dalgard contacted the animal. It was its usual curious self, nothing had alarmed or excited its interest. And he did not try to establish more than a casual contact as they made their way down the bank to the edge of the stream, Sssuri splashing in ankle-deep for the sheer pleasure of feeling liquid curl about his feet and legs once more.

Water dwellers fled from their passing and insects buzzed and hovered. Otherwise they moved through a deserted world. The stream bed widened and small islands of gravel, swept together in untidy piles by the spring floods, arose dry topped, some already showing the green of venturesome plants.

"Here—" Sssuri stopped, thrusting the butt of his spear into the shore of one such islet. He dropped cross-legged on his choice, there to remain patiently until those he sought would come with the dark. Dalgard withdrew a little way downstream and took up a similar post. The runners were shy, not easy to approach. And they would come more readily if Sssuri were alone.

Here the murmur of the stream was loud, rising above the rustle of the wind-driven grass. And the night was coming fast as the sun, hidden by the cliff wall, sank into the sea. Dalgard, knowing that his night sight was far inferior to that of the native Astran fauna, resignedly settled himself for an all-night stay, not without a second regretful memory of the snug camp by the shore.

Twilight and then night. How long before the runners would make their appearance? He could pick up the sparks of thought which marked the coming and going of hoppers, most hurrying off to their mud-plastered nests, and some-times a flicker from the mind of some other night creature. Once he was sure he touched the avid, raging hunger which marked a flying dragon, though they were not naturally hunters by darkness.

Dalgard made no move to contact Sssuri. The merman must be left undisturbed in his mental quest for the runners.

The scout lay back on his miniature island and stared up into the sky, trying to sort out all the myriad impressions of life about him. It was then that he saw it....

An arrow of fire streaking across the black bowl of Astra's night sky. A light so vivid, so alien, that it brought him to his feet with a chill prickle of apprehension along his spine. In all his years as a scout and woodsman, in all the stories of his fellows and his elders at Homeport—he had never seen, never heard of the like of that!

And through his own wonder and alert alarm, he caught Sssuri's added puzzlement.

"Danger—" The merman's verdict fed his own unease.

Danger had crossed the night, from east to west. And to the west lay what they had always feared. What was going to happen now?

2

PLANETFALL

Raf Kurbi, flitter pilot and techneer, lay on the padded shock cushion of his assigned bunk and stared with wide, disillusioned eyes at the stretch of stark, gray metal directly overhead. He tried to close his ears to the mutter of meaningless words coming from across the narrow cabin. Raf had known from the moment his name had been drawn as crew member that the whole trip would be a gamble, a wild gamble with the odds all against them. *RS 10*—those very numbers on the nose of the ship told part of the story. Ten exploring fingers thrust in turn out into the blackness of space. *RS 3*'s fate was known—she had blossomed into a pinpoint of flame within the orbit of Mars. And *RS 7* had clearly gone out of control while instruments on Terra could still pick up her broadcasts. Of the rest—well, none had returned.

But the ships were built, manned by lot from the trainees, and sent out, one every five years, with all that had been learned from the previous job, each refinement the engineers could discover incorporated into the latest to rise from the launching cradle.

RS 10—Raf closed his eyes with weary distaste. After

months of being trapped inside her ever-vibrating shell, he felt that he knew each and every rivet, seam, and plate in her only too well. And there was no reason yet to believe that the voyage would ever end. They would just go on and on through empty space until dead men manned a drifting hulk—

There—to picture that was a danger signal. Whenever his thoughts reached that particular point, Raf tried to think of something else, to break the chain of dismal foreboding. How? By joining in Wonstead's monologue of complaint and regret? Raf had heard the same words over and over so often that they no longer had any meaning—except as a series of sounds he might miss if the man who shared this pocket were suddenly stricken dumb.

"Should never have put in for training—" Wonstead's whine went up the scale.

That was unoriginal enough. They had all had that idea the minute after the sorter had plucked their names for crew inclusion. No matter what motive had led them into the stiff course of training—the fabulous pay, a real interest in the project, the exploring fever—Raf did not believe that there was a single man whose heart had not sunk when he had been selected for flight. Even he, who had dreamed all his life of the stars and the wonders which might lie just beyond the big jump, had been honestly sick on the day he had shouldered his bag aboard and had first taken his place on this mat and waited, dry mouthed and shivering, for blast-off.

One lost all sense of time out here. They ate sparingly, slept when they could, tried to while away the endless hours artificially divided into set periods. But still weeks might be months, or months weeks. They could have been years in space—or only days. All they knew was the unending monotony which dragged upon a man until he either lapsed into a dreamy rejection of his surroundings, as had Hamp and Floy, or flew into murderous rages, such as kept Morris in solitary confinement at present. And no foreseeable end to the flight—

Raf breathed shallowly. The air was stale, he could almost taste it. It was difficult now to remember being in the open air under a sky, with fresh winds blowing about one. He tried to picture on that dull strip of metal overhead a stretch of green grass, a tree, even the blue sky and floating white clouds. But the patch remained stubbornly gray, the murmur of Wonstead went on and on, a drone in his aching ears, the throb of the ship's life beat through his own thin body.

What had it been like on those legendary early flights, when the secret of the overdrive had not yet been discovered, when any who dared the path between star and star had surrendered to sleep, perhaps to wake again generations later, perhaps never to rouse again? He had seen the few documents discovered four or five hundred years ago in the raided headquarters of the scientific outlaws who had fled the regimented world government of Pax and dared space on the single hope of surviving such a journey in cold sleep, the secret of which had been lost. At least, Raf thought, they had escaped the actual discomfort of the voyage.

Had they found their new world or worlds? The end of their ventures had been debated thousands of times since those documents had been made public, after the downfall of Pax and the coming into power of the Federation of Free Men.

In fact it was the publication of the papers which had given the additional spur to the building of the *RS* armada. What man had dared once he could dare anew. And the pursuit of knowledge which had been so long forbidden under Pax was heady excitement for the world. Research and discovery became feverish avenues of endeavor. Even the slim hope of a successful star voyage and the return to Terra with such rich spoils of information was enough to harness three quarters of the planet's energy for close to a hundred years. And if the *RS 10* was not successful, there would be *11*, *12*, more—flaming into the sky and out into the void, unless some newer and more intriguing experiment developed to center public imagination in another direction.

Raf's eyes closed wearily. Soon the gong would sound and this period of rest would be officially ended. But it was hardly worth rising. He was not in the least hungry for the concentrated food. He could repeat the information tapes they carried dull word for dull word.

"Nothing to see—nothing but these blasted walls!" Again Wonstead's voice arose in querulous protest.

Yes, while in overdrive there was nothing to see. The ports of the ship would be sealed until they were in normal space once more. That is, if it worked and they were not caught up forever within this thick trap where there was no time, light, or distance.

The gong sounded, but Raf made no move to rise. He heard Wonstead move, saw from the corner of his eye the other's bulk heave up obediently from the pad.

"Hey—mess gong!" He pointed out the obvious to Raf.

With a sigh the other levered himself up on his elbows. If he did not move, Wonstead was capable of reporting him to the captain for strange behavior, and they were all too alert to a divagation which might mean trouble. He had no desire to end in confinement with Morris.

"I'm coming," Raf said sullenly. But he remained sitting on the edge of the pad until Wonstead left the cabin, and he followed as slowly as he could.

So he was not with the others when a new sound tore through the constant vibrating hum which filled the narrow corridors of the ship. Raf stiffened, the icy touch of fear tensing his muscles. Was that the red alarm of disaster?

His eyes went to the light at the end of the short passage. But no blink of warning red shown there. Not danger—then what—?

It took him a full moment to realize what he had heard, not the signal of doom, but the sound which was to herald the accomplishment of their mission—the sound which unconsciously they had all given up any hope of ever hearing. They had made it!

The pilot leaned weakly against the wall, and his eyes smarted, his hands were trembling. In that moment he knew that he had never really, honestly, believed that they would succeed. But they had! *RS 10* had reached the stars!

"Strap down for turnout—strap down for turnout—!" The disembodied voice screaming through the ship's speecher was that of Captain Hobart, but it was almost unrecognizable with emotion. Raf turned and stumbled back to his cabin, staggered to throw himself once more on his pad as he fumbled with the straps he must buckle over him.

He heard rather than saw Wonstead blunder in to follow his example, and for the first time in months the other was dumb, not uttering a word as he stowed away for the breakthrough which should take them back into normal space and the star worlds. Raf tore a nail on a fastening, muttered.

"Condition red—condition red—Strap down for breakthrough—" Hobart chanted at them from the walls. "One, two, three"—the count swung on numeral by numeral; then—"ten—Stand by—"

Raf had forgotten what breakthrough was like. He had gone through it the first time when still under take-off sedation. But this was worse than he remembered, so much worse. He tried to scream out his protest against the torture which twisted mind and body, but he could not utter even a weak cry. This, this was unbearable—a man could go mad or die—die—die....

He aroused with the flat sweetness of blood on his tongue, a splitting pain behind the eyes he tried to focus on the too familiar scrap of wall. A voice boomed, receded, and boomed again, filling the air and at last making sense, in it a ring of wild triumph!

"Made it! This is it, men, we've made it; Sol-class sun—three planets. We'll set an orbit in—"

Raf licked his lips. It was still too much to swallow in one mental gulp. So, they had made it—half of their venture was accomplished. They had broken out of their own solar system, made the big jump, and before them lay the unknown. Now it was within their reach.

"D'you hear that, kid?" demanded Wonstead, his voice no longer an accusing whine, more steady than Raf ever remembered hearing it. "We got through! We'll hit dirt again! Dirt—" his words trailed away as if he were sinking into some blissful daydream.

There was a different feeling to the ship herself. The steady drone which had ached in their ears, their bones, as she bored her way through the alien hyper-space had changed to a purr as if she, too, were rejoicing at the success of their desperate try. For the first time in weary weeks Raf remembered his own duties which would begin when the *RS 10* came in to a flame-cushioned landing on a new world. He was to assemble and ready the small exploration flyer, to man its controls and take it up and out. Frowning, he began to run over in his mind each step in the preparations he must make as soon as they planeted.

Information came down from control, where now the ports were open on normal space and the engines were under control of the spacer's pilot. Their goal was to be the third planet, one which showed signs of atmosphere, of water and earth ready and waiting.

Those who were not on flight duty crowded into the tiny central cabin, where they elbowed each other before the viewer. The ball of alien earth grew from a pinpoint to the size of an orange. They forgot time in the wonder which none had ever thought in his heart he would see on the screen. Raf knew that in control every second of this was being recorded as they began to establish a braking orbit, which with luck would bring them down on the surface of the new world.

"Cities—those must be cities!" Those in the cabin studied the plate with awe as the information filtered through the crew. Lablet, their xenobiologist, sat with his fingers rigid on the lower bar of the visa plate, so intent that nothing could break his vigil, while the rest speculated wildly. Had they really seen cities?

Raf went down the corridor to the door of the sealed compartment that held the machine and the supplies for which he was responsible. These last hours of waiting were worse with their nagging suspense than all the time which had gone before. If they could only set down!

He had, on training trips which now seemed very far in the past, trod the rust-red desert country of Mars, waddled in a bulky protective suit across the peaked ranges of the dead Moon, known something of the larger asteroids. But how would it feel to tread ground warmed by the rays of another sun? Imagination with which his superiors did not credit him began to stir. Traits inherited from a mixture of races were there to be summoned. Raf retreated once more into his cabin and sat on his bunk pad, staring down at his own capable mechanic's hands without seeing them, picturing instead all the wonders which might lie just beyond the next few hours' imprisonment in this metallic shell he had grown to hate with a dull but abiding hatred.

Although he knew that Hobart must be fully as eager as any of them to land, it seemed to Raf, and the other impatient crew members, that they were very long in entering the atmosphere of the chosen world. It was only when the order came to strap down for deceleration that they were in a measure satisfied. Pull of gravity, ship beaming in at an angle which swept it from night to day or night again as it encircled that unknown globe. They could not watch their objective any longer. The future depended entirely upon the skill of the three men in control—and last of all upon Hobart's judgment and skill.

The captain brought them down, riding the flaming counter-blasts from the ship's tail to set her on her fins in an expert point landing, so that the *RS 10* was a finger of light into the sky, amid wisps of smoke from brush ignited by her landing.

There was another wait which seemed endless to the restless men within, a wait until the air was analyzed, the countryside surveyed. But when the go-ahead signal was given and the ramp swung out, those first at the hatch still hesitated for an instant or so, though the way before them was open.

Beyond the burnt ground about the ship was a rolling plain covered with tall grass which rippled under the wind. And the freshness of that wind cleansed their lungs of the taint of the ship.

Raf pulled off his helmet, held his head high in that breeze. It was like bathing in air, washing away the smog of those long days of imprisonment. He ran down the ramp, past the little group of those who had preceded him, and fell on his knees in the grass, catching at it with his hands, a little over-awed at the wonder of it all.

The wide sweep of sky above them was not entirely blue, he noted. There was the faintest suggestion of green, and across it moved clouds of silver. But, save for the grass, they might be in a dead and empty world. Where were the cities? Or had those been born of imagination?

After a while, when the wonder of this landing had somewhat worn away, Hobart summoned them back to the prosaic business of setting up base. And Raf went to work at his own task. The sealed storeroom was opened, the supplies slung by crane down from the ship. The compact assembly, streamlined for this purpose, was all ready for the morrow.

They spent the night within the ship, much against their will. After the taste of freedom they had been given, the cramped interior weighed upon them, closing like a prison. Raf lay on his pad unable to sleep. It seemed to him that he could hear, even through the heavy plates, the sigh of that refreshing wind, the call of the open world lying ready for them. Step by step in his mind, he went through the process for which he would be responsible the next day. The uncrating of the small flyer, the assembling of frame and motor. And sometime in the midst of that survey he did fall asleep, so deeply that Wonstead had to shake him awake in the morning.

He bolted his food and was out at his job before it was far past dawn. But eager as he was to get to work, he paused just to look at the earth scuffed up by his boots, to stare for a long moment at a stalk of tough grass and remember with a thrill which never lessened that this was not native earth or grass, that he stood where none of his race, or even of his kind, had stood before—on a new planet in a new solar system.

Raf's expert training and instruction paid off. By evening he had the flitter assembled save for the motor which still reposed on the turning block. One party had gone questing out into the grass and returned with the story of a stream hidden in a gash in the plain, and Wonstead carried the limp body of a rabbit-sized furred creature he had knocked over at the waterside.

"Acted tame." Wonstead was proud of his kill. "Stupid thing just stood and watched me while I let fly with a stone."

Raf picked up the little body. Its fur was red-brown, plush-thick, and very soft to the touch. The breast was creamy white and the forepaws curiously short with an uncanny resemblance to his own hands. Suddenly he wished that Wonstead had not killed it, though he supposed that Chou, their biologist, would be grateful. But the animal looked particularly defenseless. It would have been better not to mark their first day on this new world with a killing—even if it were the knocking over of a stupid rabbit thing. The pilot was glad when Chou bore it off and he no longer had to look at it.

It was after the evening meal that Raf was called into consultation by the officers to receive his orders. When he reported that the flitter, barring unexpected accidents, would be air-borne by the following afternoon, he was shown an enlarged picture from the records made during the descent of the *RS 10.*

There was a city, right enough—showing up well from the air. Hobart stabbed a finger down into the heart of it.

"This lies south from here. We'll cruise in that direction."

Raf would have liked to ask some questions of his own. The city photographed was a sizable one. Why then this deserted land here? Why hadn't the inhabitants been out to investigate the puzzle of the space ship's landing? He said slowly, "I've mounted one gun, sir. Do you want the other installed? It will mean that the flitter can only carry three instead of four—"

Hobart pulled his lower lip between his thumb and forefinger. He glanced at his lieutenant then to Lablet, sitting quietly to one side. It was the latter who spoke first.

"I'd say this shows definite traces of retrogression." He touched the photograph. "The place may even be only a ruin."

"Very well. Leave off the other gun," Hobart ordered crisply. "And be ready to fly at dawn day after tomorrow with full field kit. You're sure she'll have at least a thousand-mile cruising radius?"

Raf suppressed a shrug. How could you tell what any machine would do under new conditions? The flitter had been put through every possible test in his home world.

Whether she would perform as perfectly here was another matter.

"They thought she would, sir," he replied. "I'll take her up for a shakedown run tomorrow after the motor is installed."

Captain Hobart dismissed him with a nod, and Raf was glad to clatter down ladders into the cool of the evening once more. Flying high in a formation of two lanes were some distant birds, at least he supposed they were birds. But he did not call attention to them. Instead he watched them out of sight, lingering alone with no desire to join those crew members who had built a campfire a little distance from the ship. The flames were familiar and cheerful, a portion, somehow, of their native world transported to the new.

Raf could hear the murmur of voices. But he turned and went to the flitter. Taking his hand torch, he checked the work he had done during the day. To-morrow—tomorrow he could take her up into the blue-green sky, circle out over the sea of grass for a short testing flight. That much he wanted to do.

But the thought of the cruise south, of venturing toward that sprawling splotch Hobart and Lablet identified as a city was somehow distasteful, and he was reluctant to think about it.

Andre Norton

3

SNAKE-DEVIL'S TRAIL

Dalgard drew the waterproof covering back over his brow, making a cheerful job of it, preparatory to their pushing out to sea once more. But he was as intent upon what Sssuri had to tell as he was on his occupation of the moment.

"But that is not even a hopper rumor," he was protesting, breaking into his companion's flow of thought.

"No. But, remember, to the runners yesterday is very far away. One night is like another; they do not reckon time as we do, nor lay up memories for future guidance. They left their native hunting grounds and are drifting south. And only a very great peril would lead the runners into such a break. It is against all their instincts!"

"So, long ago—which may be months, weeks, or just days— there came death out of the sea, and those who lived past its coming fled—" Dalgard repeated the scanty information Sssuri had won for them the night before by patient hour-long coaxing. "What kind of death?"

Sssuri's great eyes, somber and a little tired, met his. "To us there is only one kind of death to be greatly feared."

"But there are the snake-devils—" protested the colony scout.

"To be hunted down by snake-devils is death, yes. But it is a quick death, a death which can come to any living thing that is not swift or wary enough. For to the snake-devils all things that live and move are merely meat to fill the aching pit in their swollen bellies. But there were in the old days other deaths, far worse than what one meets under a snake-devil's claws and fangs. And those are the deaths we fear." He was running the smooth haft of his spear back and forth through his fingers as if testing the balance of the weapon because the time was not far away when he must rely upon it.

"Those Others!" Dalgard shaped the words with his lips as well as in his mind.

"Just so." Sssuri did not nod, but his thought was in complete agreement.

"Yet they have not come before—not since the ship of my fathers landed here," Dalgard protested, not against Sssuri's judgment but against the whole idea.

The merman got to his feet, sweeping his arm to indicate not only the cove where they now sheltered but the continent behind it.

"Once they held all this. Then they warred and killed, until but a handful lay in cover to lick their wounds and wait. It has been many threes of seasons since they left that cover. But now they come again—to loot their place of secrets— Perhaps in the time past they have forgotten much so that now they must renew their knowledge."

Dalgard stowed the bow in the bottom of the outrigger. "I

think we had better go and see," he commented, "so that we may report true tidings to our Elders—something more than rumors learned from night runners."

"That is so."

They paddled out to sea and turned the prow of the light craft north. The character of the land did not change. Cliffs still walled the coast, in some places rising sheer from the water, in others broken by a footing of coarse beach. Only flying things were to be sighted over their rocky crowns.

But by midday there was an abrupt alteration in the scene. A wide river cut through the heights and gave birth to a fan-shaped delta thickly covered with vegetation. Half hidden by the riot of growing things was a building of the dome shape Dalgard knew so well. Its windowless, doorless surface reflected the sunlight with a glassy sheen, and to casual inspection it was as untouched as it had been on the day its masters had either died within it or left it for the last time, perhaps centuries before.

"This is one way into the forbidden city," Sssuri announced. "Once they stationed guards here."

Dalgard had been about to suggest a closer inspection of the dome but that remark made him hesitate. If it had been one of the fortifications rimming in a forbidden ground, there was more than an even chance that unwary invaders, even this long after, might stumble into some trap still working automatically.

"Do we go upriver?" He left it to Sssuri, who had the traditions of his people to guide him, to make the decision.

The merman looked at the dome; it was evident from his

attitude that he had no wish to examine it more closely. "They had machines which fought for them, and sometimes those machines still fight. This river is the natural entrance for an enemy. Therefore it would have been well defended."

Under the sun the green reach of the delta had a most peaceful appearance. There was a family of duck-dogs fishing from the beach, scooping their broad bills into the mud to locate water worms. And moth birds danced in the air currents overhead. Yet Dalgard was ready to agree with his companion—beware the easy way. They dipped their paddles deep and cut across the river current toward the cliffs to the north.

Two days of steady coastwise traveling brought them to a great bay. And Dalgard gasped as the full sight of the port confronting them burst into view.

Tiers of ledges had been cut and blasted in the native rock, extending from the sea back into the land in a series of giant steps. Each of them was covered with buildings, and here the ancient war had left its mark. The rock itself had been brought to a bubbling boil and sent in now-frozen rivers down that stairway in a half-dozen places, overwhelming all structures in its path, and leaving crystallized streams to reflect the sun blindingly.

"So this is your secret city!"

But Sssuri shook his round head. "This is but the sea entrance to the country," he corrected. "Here struck the day of fire, and we need not fear the machines which doubtless lie in wait elsewhere."

They beached the outrigger and hid it in the shell of one of the ruined buildings on the lowest level. Dalgard sent out a questing thought, hoping to contact a hopper or even a duck-dog. But seemingly the ruins were bare of animal life, as was true in most of the other towns and cities he had explored in the past. The fauna of Astra was shy of any holding built by Those Others, no matter how long it may have been left to the wind, and cleansing rain.

With difficulty and detours to avoid the rivers of once-molten rock, they made their way slowly from ledge to ledge up that giant's staircase, not stopping to explore any of the buildings as they passed. There was a taint of alien age about the city which repelled Dalgard, and he was eager to get out of it into the clean countryside once more. Sssuri sped on silent feet, his shoulders hunched, his distaste for the structures to be read in every line of his supple body.

When they reached the top, Dalgard turned to gaze down to the restless sea. What a prospect! Perhaps Those Others had built thus for reasons of defense, but surely they, too, must have paused now and then to be proud of such a feat. It was the most impressive site he had yet seen, and his report of it would be a worthy addition to the Homeport records.

A road ran straight from the top of the stair, stabbing inland without taking any notice of the difficulties of the terrain, after the usual arrogant manner of the alien engineers. But Sssuri did not follow it. Instead he struck off to the left, avoiding that easy path, choosing to cross through tangles which had once been gardens or through open fields.

They were well out of the sight of the city before they flushed their first hopper, a full-grown adult with oddly pale fur. Instead of displaying the usual fearless interest in strangers, the animal took one swift look at them and fled as if a snake-devil had snorted at its thumping heels. And Dalgard received a sharp impression of terror, as if the hopper saw in him some frightening menace.

"What—?" Honestly astounded, he looked to Sssuri for enlightenment.

The hoppers could be pests. They stole any small bright object which aroused their interest. But they could also be persuaded to trade, and they usually had no fear of either colonist or merman.

Sssuri's furred face might not convey much emotion, but by all the signs Dalgard *could* read he knew that the merman was as startled as he by the strange behavior of the grass dweller.

"He is afraid of those who walk erect as we do," he made answer.

Those who walk erect—Dalgard was quick to interpret that.

He knew that Those Others were biped, quasi-human in form, closer in physical appearance to the colonists than to the mermen. And since none of Dalgard's people had penetrated this far to the north, nor had the mermen invaded this taboo territory until Sssuri had agreed to come, that left only the aliens. Those strange people whom the colonists feared without knowing why they feared them, whom the mermen hated with a hatred which had not lessened with the years of freedom. The faint rumor carried by the migrating runners must be true, for here was a hopper afraid of bipeds. And it must have been recently provided with a reason for such fear, since hoppers' memories were very short and such terror would have faded from its mind in a matter of weeks.

Sssuri halted in a patch of grass which reached to his waist belt. "It is best to wait until the hours of dark."

But Dalgard could not agree. "Better for you with your night sight," he objected, "but I do not have your eyes in my head."

Sssuri had to admit the justice of that. He could travel under the moonless sky as sure-footed as under broad sunlight. But to guide a blundering Dalgard through unknown country was not practical. However, they could take to cover and that they did as speedily as possible, using a zigzag tactic which delayed their advance but took them from one bit of protecting brush or grove of trees to the next, keeping to the fields well away from the road.

They camped that night without fire in a pocket near a spring. And while Dalgard was alert to all about them, he knew that Sssuri was mind questing in a far wider circle, trying to contact a hopper, a runner, any animal that could answer in part the inquiries they had. When Dalgard could no longer hold open weary eyes, his last waking memory was that of his companion sitting statue-still, his spear across his knees, his head leaning a trifle forward as if what he listened to was as vocal as the hum of night insects.

When the colony scout roused in the morning, his companion was stretched full length on the other side of the spring, but his head came up as Dalgard moved.

"We may go forward without fear," he shaped the assurance. "What has troubled this land has gone."

"A long time ago?"

Dalgard was not surprised at Sssuri's negative answer. "Within days *they* have been here. But they have gone once more. It will be wise for us to learn what they wanted here."

"Have they come to establish a base here once more?"

Dalgard brought into the open the one threat which had hung over his own clan since they first learned that a few of Those Others still lived—even if overseas.

"If that is their plan, they have not yet done it." Sssuri rolled over on his back and stretched. He had lost that tenseness of a hound in leash which had marked him the night before. "This was one of their secret places, holding much of their knowledge. They may return here on quest for that learning."

All at once Dalgard was conscious of a sense of urgency. Suppose that what Sssuri suggested was the truth, that Those Others were attempting to recover the skills which had brought on the devastating war that had turned this whole eastern continent into a wilderness? Equipped with even the crumbs of such discoveries, they would be enemies against which the Terran colonists could not hope to stand. The few weapons their outlaw ancestors had brought with them on their desperate flight to the stars were long since useless, and they had had no way of duplicating them. Since childhood Dalgard had seen no arms except the bows and the sword-knives carried by all venturing away from Homeport. And what use would a bow or a foot or two of sharpened metal be against things which could kill from a distance or turn rock itself into a flowing, molten river?

He was impatient to move on, to reach this city of forgotten knowledge which Sssuri was sure lay before them. Perhaps the colonists could draw upon what was stored there as well as Those Others could.

Then he remembered—not only remembered but was corrected by Sssuri. "Think not of taking *their* weapons into your hands." Sssuri did not look up as he gave that warning. "Long ago your fathers' fathers knew that the knowledge of Those Others was not for their taking."

A dimly remembered story, a warning impressed upon him during his first guided trips into the ruins near Homeport flashed into Dalgard's mind. Yes, he knew that some things had been forbidden to his kind. For one, it was best not to examine too closely the bands of color patterns which served Those Others as a means of written record. Tapes of the aliens' records had been found and stored at Homeport. But not one of the colonists had ventured to try to break the color code and learn what lay locked in those bands. Once long ago such an experiment had led to the brink of disaster, and such delvings were now considered too dangerous to be allowed.

But there was no harm in visiting this city, and certainly he must make some report to the Council about what might be taking place here, especially if Those Others were in residence or visited the site.

Sssuri still kept to the fields, avoiding the highway, until mid-morning, and then he made an abrupt turn and brought them out on the soil-drifted surface of the road. The land here was seemingly deserted. No moth birds performed their air ballets overhead, and they did not see a single hopper. That is, they did not until the road dipped before them and they started down into a cupped hollow filled with buildings. The river, whose delta they had earlier seen, made a half loop about the city, lacing it in. And here were no signs of the warfare which had ruined the port.

But in the middle of the road lay a bloody bunch of fur and splintered bone, insects busy about it. Sssuri used the point of his spear to straighten out the small corpse, displaying its headlessness. And before they reached the outer buildings of the city they found four more hoppers all mangled.

"Not a snake-devil," Dalgard deduced. As far as he knew

only the huge reptiles or their smaller flying-dragon cousins preyed upon animals. But a snake-devil would have left no remains of anything as small as a hopper, one mouthful which could not satisfy its gnawing hunger. And a flying dragon would have picked the bones clean.

"*Them*!" Sssuri's reply was clipped. "They hunt for sport."

Dalgard felt a little sick. To his mind, hoppers were to be treated with friendship. Only against the snake-devils and the flying dragons were the colonists ever at war. No wonder that hopper had run from them back on the plain during yesterday's journey!

The buildings before them were not the rounded domes of the isolated farms, but a series of upward-pointing shafts. They walked through a tall gap which must have supported a now-disappeared barrier gate, and their passing was signaled by a whispering sound as they shuffled through the loose sand and soil drifted there in a miniature dune.

This city was in a better state of preservation than any Dalgard had previously visited. But he had no desire to enter any of the gaping doorways. It was as if the city rejected him and his kind, as if to the past that brooded here he was no more than a curious hopper or a fluttering, short-lived moth bird.

"Old—old and with wisdom hidden in it—" he caught the trail of thought from Sssuri. And he was certain that the merman was no more at ease here than he himself was.

As the street they followed brought them into an open space surrounded by more imposing buildings, they made another discovery which blotted out all thoughts of forbidden knowledge and awakened them to a more normal and everyday danger.

A fountain, which no longer played but gave birth to a crooked stream of water, was in the center. And in the muddy verge of the stream, pressed deep, was the fresh track of a snake-devil. Almost full grown, Dalgard estimated, measuring the print with his fingers. Sssuri pivoted slowly, studying the circle of buildings about them.

"An hour—maybe two—" Dalgard gave a hunter's verdict on the age of the print. He, too, eyed those buildings. To meet a snake-devil in the open was one thing, to play hide-and-seek with the cunning monster in a warren such as this was something else again. He hoped that the reptile had been heading for the open, but he doubted it. This mass of buildings would provide just the type of shelter which would appeal to it for a lair. And snake-devils did not den alone!

"Try by the river," Sssuri gave advice. Like Dalgard, he accepted the necessity of the chase. No intelligent creature ever lost the chance to kill a snake-devil when fortune offered it. And he and the scout had hunted together on such trails before. Now they slipped into familiar roles from long practice.

They took a route which should lead them to the river, and within a matter of yards, came across evidence proving that the merman had guessed correctly; a second claw print was pressed deep in a patch of drifted soil.

Here the buildings were of a new type, windowless, perhaps storehouses. But what pleased Dalgard most was the fact that most of them showed tightly closed doors. There was no chance for their prey to lurk in wait.

"We should smell it." Sssuri picked that worry out of the

scout's mind and had a ready answer for it.

Sure—they should smell the lair; nothing could cloak the horrible odor of a snake-devil's home. Dalgard sniffed vigorously as he padded along. Though odd smells clung to the strange buildings none of them were actively obnoxious—yet.

"River—"

There was the river at the end of the way they had been following, a way which ended in a wharf built out over the oily flow of water. Blank walls were on either side. If the snake-devil had come this way, he had found no hiding place.

"Across the river—"

Dalgard gave a resigned grunt. For some reason he disliked the thought of swimming that stream, of having his skin laved by the turgid water with its brown sheen.

"There is no need to swim."

Dalgard's gaze followed Sssuri's pointing finger. But what he saw bobbing up and down, pulled a little downstream by the current, did not particularly reassure him. It was manifestly a boat, but the form was as alien as the city around them.

Andre Norton

4

CIVILIZATION

Raf surveyed the wide sweep of prairie where dawn gave a gray tinge to soften the distance and mark the rounded billows of the ever-rippling grass. He tried to analyze what it was about this world which made it seem so untouched, so fresh and new. There were large sections of his own Terra which had been abandoned after the Big Burn-Off and the atomic wars, or later after the counterrevolution which had defeated the empire of Pax, during which mankind had slipped far back on the road to civilization. But he had never experienced this same feeling when he had ventured into those wildernesses. Almost he could believe that the records Hobart had showed him were false, that this world had never known intelligent life herding together in cities.

He walked slowly down the ramp, drawing deep breaths of the crisp air. The day would grow warmer with the rising sun. But now it was just the sort of morning which led him to be glad he was alive—and young! Maybe part of it was because he was free of the ship and at last not just excess baggage but a man with a definite job before him.

Spacemen tended to be young. But until this moment Raf had never felt the real careless freedom of youth. Now he was moved by a desire to disobey orders—to take the flitter up by himself and head off into the blue of the brightening sky for more than just a test flight, not to explore Hobart's city but to cruise over the vast sea of grass and find out its wonders for himself.

But the discipline which had shaped him almost since birth sent him now to check the flyer and wait, inwardly impatient, for Hobart, Lablet, and Soriki, the com-tech, to join him.

The wait was not a long one since the three others, with equipment hung about, tramped down the ramp as Raf settled himself behind the control board of the flyer. He triggered the shield which snapped over them for a windbreak and brought the flitter up into the spreading color of the morning. Beside him Hobart pressed the button of the automatic recorder, and in the seat behind, Soriki had the headset of the com clamped over his ears. They were not only making a record of their trip, they were continuing in constant communication with the ship—now already a silver pencil far to the rear.

It was some two hours later that they discovered what was perhaps one reason for the isolation of the district in which the *RS 10* had set down. Rolling foothills rose beneath them and miles ahead the white-capped peaks of a mountain range made a broken outline against the turquoise sky. The broken lands would be a formidable barrier for any foot travelers: there were no easy roads through that series of sharp lifts and narrow valleys. And the one stream they followed for a short space descended from the heights in spectacular falls. Twice they skimmed thick growths of trees, so tightly packed that from the air they resembled a matted carpet of green-blue. And to cut through such a forest would be an impossible task.

The four in the flitter seldom spoke. Raf kept his attention on the controls. Sudden currents of air were tricky here, and he had to be constantly alert to hold the small flyer on an even keel. His glimpses of what lay below were only snatched ones.

At last it was necessary to zoom far above the vegetation of the lower slopes, to reach an altitude safe enough to clear the peaks ahead. Since the air supply within the windshield was constant they need not fear lack of oxygen. But Raf was privately convinced, as they soared, that the range might well compare in height with those Asian mountains which dominated all the upflung reaches of his native world.

When they were over the sharp points of that chain disaster almost overtook them. A freakish air current caught the flitter as if in a giant hand, and Raf fought for control as they lost altitude past the margin of safety. Had he not allowed for just such a happening they might have been smashed against one of the rock tips over which they skimmed to a precarious safety. Raf, his mouth dry, his hands sweating on the controls, took them up—higher than was necessary—to coast above the last of that rocky spine to see below the beginning of the downslopes leading to the plains the range cut in half. He heard Hobart draw a hissing breath.

"That was a close call." Lablet's precise, lecturer's voice cut through the drone of the motor.

"Yeah," Soriki echoed, "looked like we might be sandwich meat there for a while. The kid knows his stuff after all."

Raf grinned a little sourly, but he did not answer that. He *ought* to know his trade. Why else would he be along? They were each specialists in one or two fields. But he had good sense enough to keep his mouth shut. That way the less one had to regret minutes—or hours—later.

The land on the south side of the mountains was different in character to the wild northern plains.

"Fields!"

It did not require that identification from Lablet to point out what they had already seen. The section below was artificially divided into long narrow strips. But the vegetation growing on those strips was no different from the northern grass they had seen about the spacer.

"Not cultivated now," the scientist amended his first report. "It's reverting to grassland—"

Raf brought the flitter closer to the ground so that when a domed structure arose out of a tangle of overgrown shrubs and trees they were not more than fifty feet above it. There was no sign of life about the dwelling, if dwelling it was, and the unkempt straggle of growing things suggested that it had been left to itself through more than one season. Lablet wanted to set down and explore, but the captain was intent upon reaching the city. A solitary farm was of little value compared with what they might learn from a metropolis. So, rather to Raf's relief, he was ordered on.

He could not have explained why he shrank from such investigation. Where earlier that morning he had wanted to take the flitter and go off by himself to explore the world which seemed so bright and new, now he was glad that he was only the pilot of the flyer and that the others were not only in his company but ready to make the decisions. He had a queer distaste for the countryside, a disinclination to land near that dome.

Beyond the first of the deserted farms they came to the highway and, since the buckled and half-buried roadway ran south, Hobart suggested that they use it as a visible guide. More isolated dome houses showed in the course of an hour. And their fields were easy to map from the air. But nowhere did the Terrans see any indication that those fields were in use. Nor were there any signs of animal or bird life. The weird desolation of the landscape began to work its spell on the men in the flitter. There was something unnatural about the country, and with every mile the flyer clocked off, Raf longed to be heading in the opposite direction.

The domes drew closer together, made a cluster at crossroads, gathered into a town in which all the buildings were the same shape and size, like the cells of a wasp nest. Raf wondered if those who had built them had not been humanoid at all, but perhaps insects with a hive mind. And because that thought was unpleasant he resolutely turned his attention to the machine he piloted.

They passed over four such towns, all marking intersections of roads running east and west, north and south, with precise exactness. The sun was at noon or a little past that mark when Captain Hobart gave the order to set down so that they could break out rations and eat.

Raf brought the flitter down on the cracked surface of the road, mistrusting what might lie hidden in the field grass. They got out and walked for a space along pavement which had once been smooth.

"High-powered traffic—" That was Lablet. He had gone down on one knee and was tracing a finger along the substance.

"Straight—" Soriki squinted against the sun. "Nothing

stopped them, did it? We want a road here and we'll get it! That sort of thing. Must have been master engineers."

To Raf the straight highways suggested something else. Master engineering, certainly. But a ruthlessness too, as if the builders, who refused to accept any modifications of their original plans from nature, might be as arrogant and self-assured in other ways. He did not admire this relic of civilization; in fact it added to his vague uneasiness.

The land was so still, under the whisper of the wind. He discovered that he was listening—listening for the buzz of an insect, the squeak of some grass dweller, anything which would mean that there was life about them. As he chewed on the ration concentrate and drank sparingly from his canteen, Raf continued to listen. Without result.

Hobart and Lablet were engrossed in speculation about what might lie ahead. Soriki had gone back to the flitter to make his report to the ship. The pilot sat where he was, content to be forgotten, but eager to see an animal peering at him from cover, a bird winging through the air.

"—if we don't hit it by nightfall—But we can't be that far away! I'll stay out and try tomorrow." That was Hobart. And since he was captain what he said was probably what they would do. Raf shied away from the thought of spending the night in this haunted land. Though, on the other hand, he would be utterly opposed to lifting the flitter over those mountains again except in broad daylight.

But the problem did not arise, for they found their city in the midafternoon, the road bringing them straight to an amazing collection of buildings, which appeared doubly alien to their eyes since it did not include any of the low domes they had seen heretofore.

Andre Norton

Here were towers of needle slimness, solid blocks of almost windowless masonry looking twice as bulky beside those same towers, archways stringing at dizzy heights above the ground from one skyscraper to the next. And here time and nature had been at work. Some of the towers were broken off, a causeway displayed a gap—Once it had been a breathtaking feat of engineering, far more impressive than the highway, now it was a slowly collapsing ruin.

But before they had time to take it all in Soriki gave an exclamation. "Something coming through on our wave band, sir!" He leaned forward to dig fingers into Hobart's shoulder. "Message of some kind—I'd swear to it!"

Hobart snapped into action. "Kurbi—set down—there!"

His choice of a landing place was the flat top of a near-by building, one which stood a little apart from its neighbors and, as Raf could see, was not overlooked except by a ruined tower. He circled the flitter. The machine had been specially designed to land and take off in confined spaces, and he knew all there was possible to learn about its handling on his home world. But he had never tried to bring it down on a roof, and he was very sure that now he had no margin for error left him, not with Hobart breathing impatiently beside him, his hands moving as if, as a pilot of a spacer, he could well take over the controls here.

Raf circled twice, eyeing the surface of the roof in search of any break which could mean a crack-up at landing. And then, though he refused to be hurried by the urgency of the men with him, he came in, cutting speed, bringing them down with only a slight jar.

Hobart twisted around to face Soriki. "Still getting it?"

The other, cupping his earphones to his head with his hands, nodded. "Give me a minute or two," he told them, "and I'll have a fix. They're excited about something—the way this jabber-jabber is coming through—"

"About us," Raf thought. The ruined tower topped them to the south. And to the east and west there were buildings as high as the one they were perched on. But the town he had seen as he maneuvered for a landing had held no signs of life. Around them were only signs of decay.

Lablet got out of the flitter and walked to the edge of the roof, leaning against the parapet to focus his vision glasses on what lay below. After a moment Raf followed his example.

Silence and desolation, windows like the eye pits in bone-picked skulls. There were even some small patches of vegetation rooted and growing in pockets erosion had carved in the walls. To the pilot's uninformed eyes the city looked wholly dead.

"Got it!" Soriki's exultant cry brought them back to the flitter. As if his body was the indicator, he had pivoted until his outstretched hand pointed southwest. "About a quarter of a mile that way."

They shielded their eyes against the westering sun. A block of solid masonry loomed high in the sky, dwarfing not only the building they were standing on but all the towers around it. Its imposing lines made clear its one-time importance.

"Palace," mused Lablet, "or capitol. I'd say it was just about the heart of the city."

He dropped his glasses to swing on their cord, his eyes

glistening as he spoke directly to Raf.

"Can you set us down on that?"

The pilot measured the curving roof of the structure. A crazy fool might try to make a landing there. But he was no crazy fool. "Not on that roof!" he spoke with decision.

To his relief the captain confirmed his verdict with a slow nod. "Better find out more first." Hobart could be cautious when he wanted to. "Are they still broadcasting, Soriki?"

The com-tech had stripped the earphones from his head and was rubbing one ear. "Are they!" he exploded. "I'd think you could hear them clear over there, sir!"

And they could. The gabble-gabble which bore no resemblance to any language Terra knew boiled out of the phones.

"Someone's excited," Lablet commented in his usual mild tone.

"Maybe they've discovered us." Hobart's hand went to the weapon at his belt. "We must make peaceful contact—if we can."

Lablet took off his helmet and ran his fingers through the scrappy ginger-and-gray fringe receding from his forehead. "Yes—contact will be necessary—" he said thoughtfully.

Well, he was supposed to be their expert on that. Raf watched the older man with something akin to amusement. The pilot had a suspicion that none of the other three, Lablet included, was in any great hurry to push through contact with unknown aliens. It was a case of dancing along on shore before having to plunge into the chill of autumn sea waves.

Terrans had explored their own solar system, and they had speculated learnedly for generations on the problem of intelligent alien life. There had been all kinds of reports by experts and would-be experts. But the stark fact remained that heretofore mankind as born on the third planet of Sol had *not* encountered intelligent alien life. And just how far did speculations, reports, and arguments go when one was faced with the problem to be solved practically—and speedily?

Raf's own solution would have been to proceed with caution and yet more caution. Under his technical training he had far more imagination than any of his officers had ever realized. And now he was certain that the best course of action was swift retreat until they knew more about what was to be faced.

But in the end the decision was taken out of their hands. A muffled exclamation from Lablet brought them all around to see that distant curving roof crack wide open. From the shadows within, a flyer spiraled up into the late afternoon sky.

Raf reached the flitter in two leaps. Without orders he had the spray gun ready for action, on point and aimed at the bobbing machine heading toward them. From the earphones Soriki had left on the seat the gabble had risen to a screech and one part of Raf's brain noted that the sounds were repetitious: was an order to surrender being broadcast? His thumb was firm on the firing button of the gun and he was about to send a warning burst to the right of the alien when an order from Hobart stopped him cold.

"Take it easy, Kurbi."

Soriki said something about a "gun-happy flitter pilot," but,

Raf noted with bleak eyes, the com-tech kept his own hand close to his belt arm. Only Lablet stood watching the oncoming alien ship with placidity. But then, as Raf had learned through the long voyage of the spacer, a period of time which had left few character traits of any of the crew hidden from their fellows, the xenobiologist was a fatalist and strictly averse to personal combat.

The pilot did not leave his seat at the gun. But within seconds he knew that they had lost the initial advantage. As the tongue-shaped stranger thrust at them and then swept on to glide above their heads so that the weird shadow of the ship licked them from light to dark and then to light again, Raf was certain that his superiors had made the wrong decision. They should have left the city as soon as they picked up those signals—if they could have gone then. He studied the other flyer. Its lines suggested speed as well as mobility, and he began to doubt if they *could* have escaped with that craft trailing them.

Well, what would they do now? The alien flyer could not land here, not without coming down flat upon the flitter. Maybe it would cruise overhead as a warning threat until the city dwellers were able to reach the Terrans in some other manner. Tense, the four spacemen stood watching the graceful movements of the flyer. There were no visible portholes or openings anywhere along its ovoid sides. It might be a robot-controlled ship, it might be anything, Raf thought, even a bomb of sorts. If it was being flown by some human—or nonhuman—flyer, he was a master pilot.

"I don't understand," Soriki moved impatiently. "They're just shuttling around up there. What do we do now?"

Lablet turned his head. He was smiling faintly. "We wait," he told the com-tech. "I should imagine it takes time to climb twenty flights of stairs—if they have stairs—"

Soriki's attention fell from the flyer hovering over their heads to the surface of the roof. Raf had already looked that over without seeing any opening. But he did not doubt the truth of Lablet's surmise. Sooner or later the aliens were going to reappear. And it did not greatly matter to the marooned Terrans whether they would drop from the sky or rise from below.

Andre Norton

5

BANDED DEVIL

Familiar only with the wave-riding outriggers, Dalgard took his seat in the alien craft with misgivings. And oddly enough it also bothered him to occupy a post which earlier had served not a nonhuman such as Sssuri, whom he admired, but a humanoid whom he had been taught from childhood to avoid—if not fear. The skiff was rounded at bow and stern with very shallow sides and displayed a tendency to whirl about in the current, until Sssuri, with his instinctive knowledge of watercraft, used one of the queerly shaped paddles tucked away in the bottom to both steer and propel them. They did not strike directly across the river but allowed the current to carry them in a diagonal path so that they came out on the opposite bank some distance to the west.

Sssuri brought them ashore with masterly skill where a strip of sod angled down to the edge of the water, marking, Dalgard decided, what had once been a garden. The buildings on this side of the river were not set so closely together. Each, standing some two or three stories high, was encircled by green, as if this had been a section of private dwellings.

They pulled the light boat out of the water and Sssuri pointed at the open door of the nearest house. "In there—"

Dalgard agreed that it might be well to hide the craft against the return. Although as yet they had found no physical evidence, other than the dead hoppers, that they might not be alone in the city, he wanted a means of escape ready if such a flight would be necessary. In the meantime there was the snake-devil to track, and that wily creature, if it had swum the river, might be lurking at present in the next silent street—or miles away.

Sssuri, spear ready, was trotting along the paved lane, his head up as he thought-quested for any hint of life about them. Dalgard tried to follow that lead. But he knew that it would be Sssuri's stronger power which would warn them first.

They cast east from where they had landed, studying the soil of each garden spot, hunting for the unmistakable spoor of the giant reptile. And within a matter of minutes they found it, the mud still moist as Dalgard proved with an exploring fingertip. At the same time Sssuri twirled his spear significantly. Before them the lane ran on between two walls without any breaks. Dalgard uncased his bow and strung it. From his quiver he chose one of the powerful arrows, the points of which were kept capped until use.

A snake-devil, with its nervous system controlled not from the tiny, brainless head but from a series of auxiliary "brains" at points along its powerful spine, could and would go on fighting even after that head was shorn away, as the first colonists had discovered when they depended on the deadly ray guns fatal to any Terran life. But the poison-tipped arrow Dalgard now handled, with confidence in its complete efficiency, paralyzed within moments and killed in a quarter-hour one of the scaled monstrosities.

"Lair—"

Dalgard did not need that warning thought from his companion. There was no mistaking that sickly sweet stench born of decaying animal matter, which was the betraying effluvium of a snake-devil's lair. He turned to the right-hand wall and with a running leap reached its broad top. The lane curved to end in an archway cut through another wall, which was higher than Dalgard's head even when he stood on his present elevation. But bands of ornamental patterning ran along the taller barrier, and he was certain that it could be climbed. He lowered a hand to Sssuri and hoisted the merman up to join him.

But Sssuri stood for a long moment looking ahead, and Dalgard knew that the merman was disturbed, that the wall before them had some terrifying meaning for the native Astran. So vivid was the impression of what could only be termed horror—that Dalgard dared to ask a question:

"What is it?"

The merman's yellow eyes turned from the wall to his companion. Behind his hatred of this place there was another emotion Dalgard could not read.

"This is the place of sorrow, the place of separation. But *they* paid—oh, how they paid—after that day when the fire fell from the sky." His scaled and taloned feet moved in a little shuffling war dance, and his spear spun and quivered in the sunlight, as Dalgard had seen the spears of the mer-warriors move in the mock combats of their unexplained, and to his kind unexplainable, rituals. "Then did our spears drink, and knives eat!" Sssuri's fingers brushed the hilt of the wicked blade swinging from his belt. "Then did the People make separations and sorrows for *them*! And it was accomplished that we went forth into the sea to be no longer bond but free. And *they* went down into the darkness and were no more—" In Dalgard's head the chant of his friend skirled up in a paean of exultation. Sssuri shook his spear at the wall.

"No more the beast and the death," his thoughts swelled, a shout of victory. "For where are *they* who sat and watched many deaths? *They* are gone as the wave smashes itself upon the coast rocks and is no more. But the People are free and never more shall Those Others put bonds upon them! Therefore do I say that this is a place of nothing, where evil has turned in upon itself and come to nothing. Just as Those Others will come to nothing since their own evil will in the end eat them up!"

He strode forward along the wall until he came to the barrier, seemingly oblivious of the carrion reek which told of a snake-devil's den somewhere about. And he raised his arm high, bringing the point of his spear gratingly along the carved surface. Nor did it seem to Dalgard a futile gesture, for Sssuri lived and breathed, stood free and armed in the city of his enemies—and the city was dead.

Together they climbed the barrier, and then Dalgard discovered that it was the rim of an arena which must have seated close to a thousand in the days of its use. It was a perfect oval in shape with tiers of seats now forming a staircase down to the center, where was a section ringed about by a series of archways. A high stone grille walled this portion away from the seats as if to protect the spectators from what might enter through those portals.

Dalgard noted all this only in passing, for the arena was occupied, very much occupied. And he knew the occupiers only too well.

Three full-grown snake-devils were stretched at pulpy ease, their filled bellies obscenely round, their long necks crowned with their tiny heads flat on the sand as they napped. A pair of half-grown monsters, not yet past the six-foot stage, tore at some indescribable remnants of their elders' feasting, hissing at each other and aiming vicious blows whenever they came within possible fighting distance. Three more, not long out of their mothers' pouches scrabbled in the earth about the sleeping adults.

"A good catch," Dalgard signaled Sssuri, and the merman nodded.

They climbed down from seat to seat. This could not rightfully be termed hunting when the quarry might be picked off so easily without risk to the archer. But as Dalgard notched his first arrow, he sighted something so surprising that he did not let the poisoned dart fly.

The nearest sleeping reptile which he had selected as his mark stretched lazily without raising its head or opening its small eyes. And the sun caught on a glistening band about its short foreleg just beneath the joint of the taloned pawhands. No natural scales could reflect the light with such a brilliant glare. It could be only one thing—metal! A metal bracelet about the tearing arm of a snake-devil! Dalgard looked at the other two sleepers. One was lying on its belly with its forearms gathered under it so that he could not see if it, also, were so equipped. But the other—yes, it was banded!

Sssuri stood at the grille, one hand on its stone divisions. His surprise equaled Dalgard's. It was not in his experience either that the untamed snake-devils, regarded by merman and human alike as so dangerous as to be killed on sight, could be banded—as if they were personal pets!

For a moment or two a wild idea crossed Dalgard's mind. How long was the natural life span of a snake-devil? Until the coming of the colonists they had been the undisputed rulers of the deserted continent, stupid as they were, simply because of their strength and ferocity. A twelve-foot, scale-armored monster, that could tear apart a duocorn with ease, might not be successfully vanquished by any of the fauna of Astra. And since the monsters did not venture into the sea, contact between them and the mermen had been limited to casual encounters at rare intervals. So, how long did a snake-devil live? Were these creatures sprawled here in sleep ones that had known the domination of Those Others—though the fall of the master race of Astra must have occurred generations, hundreds of years in the past?

"No," Sssuri's denial cut through that. "The smaller one is not yet full-grown. It lacks the second neck ring. Yet it is banded."

The merman was right. That unpleasant wattle of armored flesh which necklaced the serpent throat of the devil Dalgard had picked as his target was thin, not the thick roll of fat such as distinguished its two companions. It was not fully adult, yet the band was plain to see on the foreleg now stretched to its full length as the sun bored down to supply the heavy heat the snake-devils relished next to food.

"Then—" Dalgard did not like to think of what might be the answer to that "then."

Sssuri shrugged. "It is plain that these are not wild roamers. They are here for a purpose. And that purpose—" Suddenly his arm shot out so that his fingers protruded through the slits in the stone grille. "See?"

Andre Norton

Dalgard had already seen, in seeing he knew hot and terrible anger. Out of the filthy mess in which the snake-devils wallowed, something had rolled, perhaps thrown about in play by the unspeakable offspring. A skull, dried scraps of fur and flesh still clinging to it, stared hollow-eyed up at them. At least one merman had fallen prey to the nightmares who ruled the arena.

Sssuri hissed and the red rage in his mind was plain to Dalgard. "Once more they deal death here—" His eyes went from the skull to the monsters. "Kill!" The command was imperative and sharp.

Dalgard had qualified as a master bowman before he had first gone roving. And the killing of snake-devils was a task which had been set every colonist since their first brush with the creatures.

He snapped the cap off the glass splinter point, designed to pin and then break off in the hide so that any clawing foot which tore out an arrow could not rid the victim of the poisonous head. The archer's mark was under the throat where the scales were soft and there was a chance of piercing the skin with the first shot.

The growls of the two feeding youngsters covered the snap of the bow cord as Dalgard shot. And he did not miss. The brilliant scarlet feather of the arrow quivered in the baggy roll of flesh.

With a scream which tore at the human's eardrums, the snake-devil reared to its hind feet. It made a tearing motion with the banded forearm which scraped across the back of one of its companions. And then it fell back to the blood-stained sand, limp, a greenish foam drooling from its fangs.

As the monster that the dead devil had raked roused, Dalgard had his chance for another good mark. And the second scarlet shaft sped straight to the target.

But the third creature which had been sleeping belly down on the sand presented only its armored back, a hopeless surface for an arrow to pierce. It had opened its eyes and was watching the now motionless bodies of its fellows. But it showed no disposition to move. It was almost as if it somehow understood that as long as it remained in its present position it was safe.

"The small ones—"

Dalgard needed no prompting. He picked off easily enough the two half-grown ones. The infants were another problem. Far less sluggish than their huge elders they sensed that they were in danger and fled. One took refuge in the pouch of its now-dead parent, and the others moved so fast that Dalgard found them difficult targets. He killed one which had almost reached an archway and at length nicked the second in the foot, knowing that, while the poison would be slower in acting, it would be as sure.

Through all of this the third adult devil continued to lie motionless, only its wicked eyes giving any indication that it was alive. Dalgard watched it impatiently. Unless it would move, allow him a chance to aim at the soft underparts, there was little chance of killing it.

What followed startled both hunters, versed as they were in the usual mechanics of killing snake-devils. It had been an accepted premise, through the years since the colonists had known of the monsters, that the creatures were relatively brainless, mere machines which fought, ate, and killed, incapable of any intelligent reasoning, and therefore only

Andre Norton

dangerous when one was surprised by them or when the hunter was forced to face them inadequately armed.

This snake-devil was different, as it became increasingly plain to the two behind the grille. It had remained safe during the slaughter of its companions because it had not moved, almost as if it had wit enough *not* to move. And now, when it did change position, its maneuvers, simple as they were, underlined the fact that this one creature appeared to have thought out a solution to its situation—as rational a solution as Dalgard might have produced had it been his problem.

Still keeping its soft underparts covered, it edged about in the sand until its back, with the impenetrable armor plates, was facing the grille behind which the hunters stood. Retracting its neck between its shoulders and hunching its powerful back limbs under it, it rushed from that point of danger straight for one of the archways.

Dalgard sent an arrow after it. Only to see the shaft scrape along the heavy scales and bounce to the sand. Then the snake-devil was gone.

"Banded—" The word reached Dalgard. Sssuri had been cool enough to note that while the human hunter had been only bewildered by the untypical actions of his quarry.

"It must be intelligent." The scout's statement was more than half protest.

"Where *they* are concerned, one may expect many evil wonders."

"We've got to get that devil!" Dalgard was determined on that. Though to run down, through this maze of deserted city, an enraged snake-devil—above all, a snake-devil which appeared to have some reasoning powers—was not a prospect to arouse any emotion except grim devotion to duty.

"It goes for help."

Dalgard, startled, stared at his companion. Sssuri was still by the grille, watching that archway through which the devil had disappeared.

"What kind of help?" For a moment Dalgard pictured the monster returning at the head of a regiment of its kind, able to tear out this grille and get at their soft-fleshed enemies behind it.

"Safety—protection," Sssuri told him. "And I think that the place to which it now flees is one we should know."

"Those Others?" The sun had not clouded, it still streamed down in the torrid heat of early afternoon, warm on their heads and shoulders. Yet Dalgard felt as chill as if some autumn wind had laid its lash across the small of his back.

"*They* are not here. But they have been—and it is possible that they return. The devil goes to where it expects to find them."

Sssuri was already on his way, running about the arena's curve to reach the point above the archway through which the snake-devil had raced. Dalgard padded after him, bow in hand. He trusted Sssuri implicitly when it came to tracking. If the merman said that the snake-devil had a definite goal in view, he was right. But the scout was still a little bemused by a monster who was able to have any goal except the hunting and devouring of meat. Either the one who fled was a freak among its kind or—There were several possibilities which could answer that "or," and none of them were very pleasant to consider.

They reached the section above the archway and climbed the tiers of seat benches to the top of the wall. Only to see no exit below them. In fact nothing but a wide sweep of crushed brown tangle which had once been vegetation. It was apparent that there was no door below.

Sssuri sped down again. He climbed the grille and was on his way to the sand when Dalgard caught up with him. Together they ventured into the underground passage which the snake-devil had chosen.

The stench of the lair was thick about them. Dalgard coughed, sickened by the foul odor. He was reluctant to advance. But, to his growing relief, he discovered that it was not entirely dark. Set in the roof at intervals were plates which gave out a violet light, making a dim twilight which was better than total darkness.

It was a straight passage without any turns or openings. But the horrible odor was constant, and Dalgard began to think that they might be running head-on into another lair, perhaps one as well populated as that they had left behind them. It was against nature for the snake-devils he had known to lair under cover; they preferred narrow rocky places where they could bask in the sun. But then the devil they now pursued was no ordinary one.

Sssuri reassured him. "There is no lair, only the smell because they have come this way for many years."

The passage opened into a wide room and here the violet light was stronger, bright enough to make plain the fact that alcoves opened off it, each and every one with a barred grille for a door. There was no mistaking that once this had been a prison of sorts.

Sssuri did no exploring but crossed the room at his shuffling trot, which Dalgard matched. The way leading out on the opposite side slanted up, and he judged it might bring them out at ground level.

"The devil waits," Sssuri warned, "because it fears. It will turn on us when we come. Be ready—"

They were at another door, and before them was a long corridor with tall window openings near the ceiling which gave admittance to the sunlight. After the gloom of the tunnel, Dalgard blinked. But he was aware of movement at the far end, just as he heard the hissing scream of the monster they trailed.

6

TREASURE HUNT

Raf, squatting on a small, padded platform raised some six inches from the floor, tried to study the inhabitants of the room without staring offensively. At the first glance, in spite of their strange clothing and their odd habit of painting their faces with weird designs, the city people might have been of his own species. Until one saw their too slender hands with the three equal-length fingers and thumb, or caught a glimpse, under the elaborate head coverings, of the stiff, spiky substance which served them for hair.

At least they did not appear to be antagonistic. When they had reached the roof top where the Terrans had landed their flitter, they had come with empty hands, making gestures of good will and welcome. And they had had no difficulty in persuading at least three of the exploring party to accompany them to their own quarters, though Raf had been separated from the flyer only by the direct order of Captain Hobart, an order he still resented and wanted to disobey.

The Terrans had been offered refreshment—food and drink. But knowing the first rule of stellar exploration, they had refused, which did not mean that the hosts must abstain. In fact, Raf thought, watching the aliens about him, they ate as if such a feast were novel. His two neighbors had quickly divided his portion between them and made it disappear as fast, if not faster, than their own small servings.

At the other end of the room Lablet and Hobart were trying to communicate with the nobles about them, while Soriki, a small palm recorder in his hand, was making a tape strip of the proceedings.

Raf glanced from one of his neighbors to the other. The one on his right had chosen to wear a sight-torturing shade of crimson, and the material was wound in strips about his body as if he were engulfed in an endless bandage. Only his fluttering hands, his three-toed feet and his head were free of the supple rolls. Having selected red for his clothing, he had picked a brilliant yellow paint for his facial makeup, and it was difficult for the uninitiated to trace what must be his normal features under that thick coating of stuff which fashioned a masklike strip across his eyes and a series of circles outlining his mouth, circles which almost completely covered his beardless cheeks. More twists of woven fabric, opalescent and changing color as his head moved, made a turban for his head.

Most of the aliens about the room wore some variation of the same bandage dress, face paint, and turban. An exception, one of three such, was the feaster on Raf's left.

His face paint was confined to a conservative set of bars on each cheek, those a stark black and white. His sinewy arms were bare to the shoulder, and he wore a shell of some metallic substance as a breast-and back-plate, not unlike the very ancient body armor of Raf's own world. The rest of his body was covered by the bandage strips, but they were of a dead black, which, because of the natural thinness of his limbs, gave him a rather unpleasant resemblance to a spider.

Various sheaths and pockets hung from a belt pulled tight about his wasp middle, and a helmet of the metal covered his head. Soldier? Raf was sure that his guess was correct.

The officer, if officer he was, caught Raf's gaze. His small round mouth gaped, and then his hands, with a few quick movements which Raf followed, fascinated, pantomimed a flyer in the air. With those talking fingers, he was able to make plain a question: was Raf the pilot of the flitter?

The pilot nodded. Then he pointed to the officer and forced as inquiring an expression as he could command.

The answer was sketched quickly and readably: the alien, too, was either a pilot or had some authority over flyers. For the first time since he had entered this building, Raf knew a slight degree of relaxation.

The wrinkleless, too smooth skin of the alien was a darkish yellow. His painted face was a mask to frighten any sensible Terran child; his general appearance was not attractive. But he was a flyer, and he wanted to talk shop, as well as they could with no common speech. Since the scarlet-wound nobleman on Raf's right was completely engrossed in the feast, pursuing a few scraps avidly about the dish, the Terran gave all his attention to the officer.

Twittering words poured in a stream from the warrior's lips. Raf shook his head regretfully, and the other jerked his shoulders in almost human impatience. Somehow that heartened Raf.

With many guesses to cover gaps, probably more than half of which were wrong, Raf gathered that the officer was one of a very few who still retained the almost forgotten knowledge of how to pilot the remaining airworthy craft in this crumbling city. On their way to the building with the curved roof, Raf had noted the evidences that the inhabitants of this metropolis could not be reckoned as more than a handful and that most of these now lived either within the central building or close to it. A pitiful collection of survivors lingering on in the ruins of their past greatness.

Yet he was impressed now by no feeling that the officer, eagerly trying to make contact, was a degenerate member of a dying race. In fact, as Raf glanced at the aliens about the room, he was conscious of an alertness, of a suppressed energy which suggested a young and vigorous people.

The officer was now urging him to go some place, and Raf, his dislike for being in the heart of the strangers' territory once more aroused, was about to shake his head in a firm negative when a second idea stopped him. He had resisted separation from the flitter. Perhaps he could persuade the alien, under the excuse of inspecting a strange machine, to take him back to the flyer. Once there he would stay. He did not know what Captain Hobart and Lablet thought they could accomplish here. But, as for himself, Raf was sure that he was not going to feel easy again until he was across the northern mountain chain and coming in for a landing close by the *RS 10*.

It was as if the alien officer had read his thoughts, for the warrior uncrossed his black legs and got nimbly to his feet with a lithe movement, which Raf, cramped by sitting in the unfamiliar posture, could not emulate. No one appeared to notice their withdrawal. And when Raf hesitated, trying to catch Hobart's eye and make some explanation, the alien touched his arm lightly and motioned toward one of the curtained doorways. Conscious that he could not withdraw from the venture now, Raf reluctantly went out.

They were in a hall where bold bands of color interwove in patterns impossible for Terran eyes to study. Raf lowered his gaze hurriedly to the gray floor under his boots. He had discovered earlier that to try to trace any thread of that wild splashing did weird things to his eyesight and awakened inside him a sick panic. His space boots, with the metal, magnetic plates set in the soles, clicked loudly on the pavement where his companion's bare feet made no whisper of sound.

The hall gave upon a ramp leading down, and Raf recognized this. His confidence arose. They were on their way out of the building. Here the murals were missing so that he could look about him for reference points.

He was sure that the banquet hall was some ten stories above street level. But they did not go down ten ramps now. At the foot of the third the officer turned abruptly to the left, beckoning Raf along. When the Terran remained stubbornly where he was, pointing in the direction which, to him, meant return to the flitter, the other made gestures describing an aircraft in flight. His own probably.

Raf sighed. He could see no way out unless he cut and ran. And long before he reached the street from this warren they could pick him up. Also, in spite of all the precautions he had taken to memorize their way here, he was not sure he could find his path back to the flyer, even if he were free to go. Giving in, he went after the officer.

Their way led out on one of the spider-web bridges which tied building and tower into the complicated web which was the city. Raf, as a pilot of flitter, had always believed that he had no fear of heights. But he discovered that to coast above the ground in a flyer was far different than to hurry at the pace his companion now set across one of these narrow bridges suspended high above the street. And he was sure that the surface under them vibrated as if the slightest extra poundage would separate it from its supports and send it, and them, crashing down.

Luckily the distance they had to cover was relatively short, but Raf swallowed a sigh of relief as they reached the door at the other end. They were now in a tower which, unluckily, proved to be only a way station before another swing out over empty space on a span which sloped down! Raf clutched at the guide rail, the presence of which suggested that not all the users of this road were as nonchalant as the officer who tripped lightly ahead. This must explain the other's bare feet—on such paths they were infinitely safer than his own boots.

The downward sloping bridge brought them to a square building which somehow had an inhabited look which those crowding around it lacked. Raf gained its door to become aware of a hum, a vibration in the wall he touched to steady himself, hinting at the drive of motors, the throb of machinery inside the structure. But within, the officer passed along a corridor to a ramp which brought them out, after what was for Raf a steep climb, upon the roof. Here was not one of the tongue-shaped craft such as had first met them in the city, but a gleaming globe. The officer stopped, his eyes moving from the Terran to the machine, as if inviting Raf to share in his own pride. To the pilot's mind it bore little resemblance to any form of aircraft past or present with which he had had experience in his own world. But he did not doubt that it was the present acme of alien construction, and he was eager to see it perform.

He followed the officer through a hatch at the bottom of the globe, only to be confronted by a ladder he thought at first he could not climb, for the steps were merely toe holds made to accommodate the long, bare feet of the crew. By snapping on the magnetic power of his space boots, Raf was able to get up, although at a far slower speed than his guide. They passed several levels of cabins before coming out in what was clearly the control cabin of the craft.

To Raf the bank of unfamiliar levers and buttons had no meaning, but he paid strict attention to the gestures of his companion. This was not a space ship he gathered. And he doubted whether the aliens had ever lifted from their own planet to their neighbors in this solar system. But it was a long-range ship with greater cruising power than the other flyer he had seen. And it was being readied now for a voyage of some length.

The Terran pilot squatted down on the small stool before the controls. Before him a visa plate provided a clear view of the sky without and the gathering clouds of evening. Raf shifted uncomfortably. That signal of the passing of time triggered his impatience to be away—back to the *RS 10*. He did not want to spend the night in this city. Somehow he must get the officer to take him back to the flitter—to be there would be better than shut up in one of the alien dwellings.

Meanwhile he studied the scene on the visa plate, trying to find the roof on which they had left the flitter. But there was no point he was able to recognize.

Raf turned to the officer and tried to make clear the idea of returning to his own ship. Either he was not as clever at the sign language as the other, or the alien did not wish to understand. For when they left the control cabin, it was only to make an inspection tour of the other parts of the globe, including the space which held the motors of the craft and which, at another time, would have kept Raf fascinated for hours.

In the end the Terran broke away and climbed down the thread of ladder to stand on the roof under the twilight sky. Slowly he walked about the broad expanse of the platform, attempting to pick out some landmark. The central building of the city loomed high, and there were any number of towers about it. But which was the one that guarded the roof where the flitter rested? Raf's determination to get back to his ship was a driving force.

The alien officer had watched him, and now a three-fingered hand was laid on Raf's sleeve while its owner looked into Raf's face and mouthed a trilling question.

Without much hope the pilot sketched the set of gestures he had used before. And he was surprised when the other led the way down into the building. This time they did not go back to the bridge, which had brought them across the canyons of streets, but kept on down ramps within the building.

There was a hum of activity in the place. Aliens, all in tight black wrappings and burnished metal breastplates, their faces barred with black and white paint, went on errands through the halls or labored at tasks Raf could not understand. It now seemed as if his guide were eager to get him away.

It was when they reached the street level that the officer did pause by one door, beckoning Raf imperiously to join him. The Terran obeyed reluctantly—and was almost sick.

He was staring down at a dead, very dead body. By the stained rags still clinging to it, it was one of the aliens, a noble, not one of the black-clad warriors. The gaping wounds which had almost torn the unfortunate apart were like nothing Raf had ever seen.

With a guttural sound which expressed his feelings as well as any words, the officer picked up from the floor a broken spear, the barbed head of which was dyed the same reddish yellow as the blood still seeping from the torn body. Swinging the weapon so close to Raf that the Terran was forced to retreat a step or two to escape contact with the grisly relic, the officer burst into an impassioned speech. Then he went back to the gestures which were easier for the spaceman to understand.

This was the work of a deadly enemy, Raf gathered. And such a fate awaited any one of them who ventured beyond certain bounds of safety. Unless this enemy were destroyed, the city—life itself—was no longer theirs—

Seeing those savage wounds which suggested that an insane fury had driven the attacker, Raf could believe that. But surely a primitive spear was no equal to the weapons his guide could command.

When he tried to suggest that, the other shook his head as if despairing of making plain his real message, and again beckoned Raf to come with him. They were out on the littered street, heading away from the central building where the rest of the Terran party must still be. And Raf, seeing the lengthening shadows, the pools of dusk gathering, and remembering that spear, could not resist glancing back over his shoulder now and then. He wondered if the metallic click of his boot soles on the pavement might not draw attention to them, attention they would not care to meet. His hand was on his stun gun. But the officer gave no sign of being worried; he walked along with the assurance of one who has nothing to fear.

Then Raf caught sight of a patch of color he had seen before and relaxed. They *were* on their way back to the flitter! He had come down this very street earlier. And he did not mind the long climb back, ramp by steep ramp, which brought him out at last beside the flyer. His relief was so great that he put out his hand to draw it along the sleek side of the craft as he might have caressed a well-loved pet.

"Kurbi?"

At Hobart's bark he stiffened. "Yes, sir!"

"We camp here tonight. Have to make some plans."

"Yes, sir." He agreed with that. To attempt passage of the mountains in the dark was a suicide mission which he would have refused. On the other hand, to his mind, they would sleep more soundly if they were out of the city. He speculated whether he dared suggest that they use the few remaining moments of twilight to head into the open and establish a camp somewhere in the countryside.

The alien officer made some comment in his slurred speech and faded away into the shadows. Raf saw that the others had already dragged out their blanket rolls and were spreading them in the shelter of the flitter while Soriki busied himself at the com, sending back a message to the *RS 10*.

"... should not be too difficult to establish a common speech form," Lablet was saying as Raf climbed into the flitter to tug loose his own roll. "Color and pitch both seem to carry meaning. But the basic pattern is there to study. And with the scanner to sort out those record strips—did you adjust them, Soriki?"

"They're all ready for you to push the button. If the scanner can read them, it will. I got all that speech the chief, or king, or whatever he was, made just before we left."

"Good, very good!" In the light of the portable lamp by Soriki's com, Lablet settled down, plugged the scanner tubes in his ears, absently accepting a ration bar the captain handed him to chew on while he listened to the playback of the record the com-tech had made that afternoon.

Hobart turned to Raf. "You went off with that officer. What did he have to show you?"

The pilot described the globe and the body he had been shown and then added what he had deduced from the sketchy explanations he had been given. The captain nodded.

"Yes, they have aircraft, have been using them, too. But I think that there's only one of the big ones. And they're fighting a war all right. We didn't see the whole colony, but I'll wager that there are only a handful of them left. They're holed up here, and they need help or the barbarians will finish them off. They talked a lot about that."

Lablet pulled the ear plugs from his ears. In the lamplight there was an excited expression on his face. "You were entirely right, Captain! They were offering us a bargain there at the last! They are offering us the accumulated scientific knowledge of this world!"

"What?" Hobart sounded bewildered.

"Over there"—Lablet made a sweep with his arm which might indicate any point to the east—"there is a storehouse of the original learning of their race. It's in the heart of the enemy country. But the enemy as yet do not know of it. They've made two trips over to bring back material and their ship can only go once more. They offer us an equal share if we'll make the next trip in their company and help them clean out the storage place—"

Hobart's answer was a whistle. There was an avid hunger on Lablet's lean face. No more potent bribe could have been devised to entice him. But Raf, remembering the spear-torn body, wondered.

In the heart of the enemy country, he repeated to himself.

Lablet added another piece of information. "After all, the enemy they face is only dangerous because of superior numbers. They are only animals—"

"Animals don't carry spears!" Raf protested.

"Experimental animals that escaped during a world-wide war generations ago," reported the other. "It seems that the species have evolved to a semi-intelligent level. I must see them!"

Hobart was not to be hurried. "We'll think it over," he decided. "This needs a little time for consideration."

7

MANY EYES, MANY EARS

This was not the first time Dalgard had faced the raging fury of a snake-devil thirsting for a kill. The slaying he had done in the arena was an exception to the rule, not the usual hunter's luck. And now that he saw the creature crouched at the far end of the hall he was ready. Sssuri, also, followed their familiar pattern, separating from his companion and slipping along the wall toward the monster, ready to attract its attention at the proper moment.

Only one doubt remained in Dalgard's mind. This devil had not acted in the normal brainless fashion of its kin. What if it was able to assess the very simple maneuvers, which always before had completely baffled its species, and attacked not the moving merman but the waiting archer?

It was backed against another door, a closed one, as if it had fled for refuge to some aid it had expected and did not find. But as Sssuri moved, its long neck straightened until it was almost at right angles with its narrow shoulders, and from its snake's jaws proceeded a horrific hissing which arose to a scream as its leg muscles tensed for a spring.

At just the right moment Sssuri's arm went back, his spear

sang through the air. And the snake-devil, with an incredible twist of its neck, caught the haft of the weapon between its teeth, crunching the iron-hard substance into powder. But with that move it exposed its throat, and the arrow from Dalgard's bow was buried head-deep in the soft inner flesh.

The snake-devil spat out the spear and tried to raise its head. But the muscles were already weakening. It fought the poison long enough to take a single step forward, its small red eyes alight with brainless hate. Then it crashed and lay twisting. Dalgard lowered his bow. There was no need for a second shot.

Sssuri regarded the remains of his spear unhappily. Not only was it the product of long hours of work, but no merman ever felt fully equipped to face the world without such a weapon to hand. He salvaged the barbed head and broke it free of the shred of haft the snake-devil had left. Knotting it at his belt he turned to Dalgard.

"Shall we see what lies beyond?"

Dalgard crossed the hall to test the door. It did not yield to an inward push, but rolled far enough into the wall to allow them through.

On the other side was a room which amazed the scout. The colonists had their laboratory, their workshops, in which they experimented and tried to preserve the remnants of knowledge their forefathers had brought across space, as well as to discover new. But the extent of this storehouse with its bewildering mass of odd machines, tanks, bales, and stocked shelves and tables, was too much to be taken in without a careful and minute examination.

"We are not the first to walk here." Sssuri had given little attention to what was stacked about him. Instead he bent over the disturbed dust in one aisle. Dalgard noted as he went to join the merman that there were gaps on those tables which ran the full length of the room, lines left in the grimy deposit of years which told of things recently moved. And then he saw what had interested Sssuri: tracks, some resembling those which his own bare feet might leave, except that there were only three toes!

"*They.*"

Dalgard who had been a hunter and a tracker before he was an explorer crouched for a clearer view. Yes, they were recent, yet not made today or even yesterday; there was a thin film of dust resettled in each.

"Some days ago. They are not in the city now," the merman declared with certainty. "But they will come again."

"How do you know that?"

Sssuri's hand swept about to include the wealth around them. "They have taken some, perhaps to them the most needful. But they will not be able to resist gathering the rest. Surely they will return, perhaps not once but many times. Until—"

"Until they come to stay." Dalgard was grim as he completed that sentence for the other.

"That is what they will work for. This land was once under their mastery. This world was theirs before they threw it away warring among themselves. Yes, they dream of holding all once more. But"—Sssuri's yellow eyes took on some of the fire which had shone in those of the snake-devil during its last seconds of life—"that must not be so!"

"If they take the land, you have the sea," Dalgard pointed out. The mermen had a means of escape. But what of his own clansmen? Large families were unknown among the Terran colonists. In the little more than a century they had been on this planet their numbers, from the forty-five survivors of the voyage, had grown to only some two hundred and fifty, of which only a hundred and twenty were old enough or young enough to fight. And for them there was no retreat or hiding place.

"We do not go bask to the depths!" There was stern determination in that declaration from Sssuri. His tribe had been long hunted, and it wasn't until they had made a loose alliance with the Terran colonists that they had dared to leave the dangerous ocean depths, where they were the prey of monsters more ferocious and cunning than any snake-devil, to house their families in the coast caves and on the small islands off-shore, to increase in numbers and develop new skills of civilization. No, knowing the stubbornness which was bred into their small, furry bodies, Dalgard did not believe that many of the sea people would willingly go back into the sunless depths. They would not surrender tamely to the rulership of the loathed race.

"I don't see," Dalgard spoke aloud, half to himself, as he studied the tables closely packed, the machines standing on bases about the walls, the wealth of alien technology, "what we can do to stop them."

The restriction drilled into him from early childhood, that the knowledge of Those Others was not for his race and in some way dangerous, gave him an uneasy feeling of guilt just to be standing there. Danger, danger which was far worse than physical, lurked there. And he could bring it to life by merely putting out his hand and picking up any one of those fascinating objects which lay only inches away. For the pull of curiosity was warring inside him against the stern warnings of his Elders.

Once when Dalgard had been very small he had raided his father's trip bag after the next to the last exploring journey the elder Nordis had made. And he had found a clear block of some kind of greenish crystal, in the heart of which threadlike lines of color wove patterns which were utterly strange. When he had turned the block in his hand, those lines had whirled and changed to form new and intricate designs. And when he had watched them intently it had seemed that something happened inside his mind and he knew, here and there, a word, a fragment of alien thought— just as he normally communicated with the cub who was Sssuri or the hoppers of the field. And his surprise had been so great that he had gone running to his father with the cube and the story of what happened when one watched it.

But there had been no praise for his discovery. Instead he had been hurried off to the chamber where an old, old man, the son of the Great Man who had planned to bring them across space, lay in his bed. And Forken Kordov himself had talked to Dalgard in his old voice, a voice as withered and thin as the hands crossed helplessly on his shrunken body, explaining in simple, kindly words that the knowledge which lay in the cubes, in the oddly shaped books which the Terrans sometimes came across in the ruins, was not for them. That his own great-grandfather Dard Nordis, who had been one of the first of the mutant line of sensitives, had discovered that. And Dalgard, impressed by Forken, by his father's concern, and by all the circumstances of that day, had never forgotten nor lost that warning.

"*We* cannot hope to stop them," Sssuri pointed out. "But we must learn when they will come again and be waiting for them—with your people and mine. For I tell you now, brother of the knife, they must not be allowed to rise once more!"

"And how can we foretell their coming?" Dalgard wanted to know.

"Perhaps that alone we cannot do. But when they come they will not leave speedily. They have stayed here before without harm, and their distrust has been lulled. When next they come, it will be only according to their natures that they will wish to stay longer. Not snatching up the closest to hand of these treasures of theirs, but choosing out with care those things which will give them the best results. Therefore they may make a camp, and we can summon others to aid us."

"To return to Homeport will take several days even if we push," pointed out the scout.

"Word can pass swifter than man," the merman returned, with confidence in his own plan of action. "We shall put other eyes, other ears, many eyes, many ears, to service for us. Be assured we are not the only ones to fear the return of Those Others from overseas."

Dalgard caught his meaning. Yes, it would not be the first time the hoppers and other small animals living in the grasslands, the runners and even the moth birds that only the mermen could mind touch, would relay a message across the land. It might not be an accurate message—to transmit that by small animal brains was impossible—but the meaning would reach both merman and colony Elders: trouble in the north, help needed there. And since Dalgard was the only explorer at present who had chosen the northern trails, his people would know that he had sent that warning and would act upon it, as Sssuri's message would in turn be heeded by the warriors of his tribe.

Yes, it could be done. But what of the traces they had left here—the slaughtered snake-devils—?

Sssuri had an answer for that also. "Let them believe that one of my race came here, or that a party of us ventured to explore inland. We can make it appear that way. But they must not know of you. I do not believe that they ever learned of you or how your fathers came from the sky. And so that may swing the battle in our favor if it comes to open warfare."

What the merman said was sensible enough, and Dalgard was willing to obey orders. As he left the storehouse, Sssuri trailed him, scuffing each dusty print the scout left. Perhaps a master of trailcraft could unravel that spoor, but the colonist was ready to believe that no such master existed in the ranks of Those Others.

In the outer hall the merman approached the now dead snake-devil and jerked from its loose skin the arrow which had killed it. Loosing the head of his ruined spear from his belt, he dug and gouged at the small wound, tearing it so that its original nature was concealed forever. Then they retraced their way through the underground passages until they reached the sanded arena. Already insects buzzed hungrily about the hulks of the dead monsters.

There was a shrill squeal as the remaining infant reptile fled from the pouch where it had hidden. Sssuri hurled his knife, and the blade caught the small devil above the shoulder line, half cutting, half snapping its tender neck, so that it bounded aimlessly on to crash against the wall and fall back squirming feebly.

They collected the darts which had killed the others. Dalgard took the opportunity to study those bands on the forearms of the adults. To his touch they had the slick smoothness of metal, yet he was unfamiliar with the material. It possessed the ruddy fire of copper, but through it ran small black veins. He would have liked to have taken one with him for investigation, but it was out of the question to pry it off that scaled limb.

Sssuri straightened up from his last gruesome bit of stage-setting with a sigh of relief. "Go ahead." He pointed to one of the other archways. "I will confuse the trail."

Dalgard obeyed, treading as lightly as he could, avoiding all stretches in which he could leave a clear print. Sssuri ran lightly back and forth mixing the few impressions to the best of his ability.

They backtracked to the river, retrieved the boat and recrossed, to leave the city behind and strike into the open country beyond its sinister walls. Night was falling, and Dalgard was very glad that he was not to spend the time of darkness within those haunted buildings. But he knew that it was more than a dislike for being shut up in the alien dwellings which had brought Sssuri out into the fields. The second part of their plan must be put into operation.

While Dalgard willed his body motionless, the merman lay relaxed upon the ground before him as he might have floated upon his beloved waves in some secluded cove. His brilliant eyes were closed. Yet Dalgard knew that Sssuri was far from asleep, and with all his own power he tried to join in the broadcast: that urgency which should send some hopper, some night runner, on to spread the rumor that there was trouble in the north, that danger existed and must be investigated. They had already met one colony of runners ranging southward to escape. But if they could send another such tribe traveling, arouse and aim south a hopper exodus, the story would spread until the fringe would reach the animals who lived in peace within touch of Homeport.

The sun was gone, the dark gathered fast. Dalgard could not even see the clustered buildings of the city now. And since he lacked Sssuri's range and staying power, he had no idea whether their efforts had met with even a shadow of success. He shivered in the bite of the wind and dared to lay his hand on Sssuri's shoulder, feeling anew the electric shock of warmth and bursting life which was always there.

Having so broken the other's absorption he asked a question: "Would it not be well, brother of the knife, if with the rising sun you returned to the sea and struck out to join your tribesmen, leaving me here to watch until you return?"

Sssuri's answer came with a speed which suggested that he, too, had been considering that problem. "We shall see what happens with the sun's rising. It is true that in the sea I can travel with greater speed, that there are hunting parties of my people striking into these waters. But they will not come to this city without good reason. It is an accursed place."

With the early morning the city drew them once more. Dalgard's curiosity pulled him to that storehouse. He could not stifle the hope that with luck he might find something there which would solve their problem for them. If there could only be a way to avoid open conflict with Those Others, some solution whereby the aliens need never know of the existence of the Colony. For so many generations, even centuries, the aliens had been confined, or had confined themselves, safely overseas on the western continent. Perhaps if now they were faced by some new catastrophe, they would never attempt to come east again. He had visions of discovering and activating some trap set to protect their treasures which could be turned against them. But he realized that he lacked the technical knowledge which would have aided him in the search for such a weapon.

The remnants of Terran science and mechanics, which the outlaws had brought with them from their native world, had been handed on; the experiments they had managed since with crude equipment had been carefully recorded, and he was acquainted with the outlines of most of them. But the few destructive arms they had imported were long since worn out or lacked charges, and they had not been able to duplicate them. Just as they had torn asunder the ship in which they had crossed space, to use its parts for the building of Homeport, so had they hoarded all else they had brought. But they were limited by lack of materials on Astra, and their fear of the knowledge of the aliens had kept them from experimenting with things found in the ruins.

There might be hundreds of objects on the shelves of that storage place, which, properly used, would reduce not only just the room and its contents to glowing slag, but take half the city with it. But he had no idea which, or which combination, would do it.

And here Sssuri could be no help. The mermen had made great strides forward in biological and mental sciences, but mechanics was a closed section of learning because of their enforced habitat under the sea, and of machines they knew less than the colonists.

"I have been thinking—" Sssuri broke into his companion's chain of reasoning, "of what we may do. And perhaps there is a way to reach the sea more swiftly than by returning overland."

"Downriver? But you said that way may have its watching devices."

"Which would be centered on objects coming upstream, not down. But in this city there should be yet another way—"

He did not enlarge upon that, but since he apparently knew what he was doing, Dalgard let him play guide once more. They recrossed the sluggish river, the scout looking into its murky depths with little relish for it as a means of transportation. Though it had an oily, flowing current, there was a suggestion of stagnant water with unpleasant surprises waiting beneath its turgid surface.

For the second time they entered the arena. Avoiding the bodies, Sssuri made a circuit of the sanded floor. He did not turn in at the archway which led to the storage place, but paused before another as if there lay what he had been searching for.

Dalgard's less sensitive nostrils picked up a new scent, the not-to-be-missed fetor of damp underground ways where water stood. The merman edged around a barred gate as Dalgard sniffed again. The smell of damp was crossed by other and even less appetizing odors, but he did not catch the stench of the snake-devils. And, relying on Sssuri's judgment, he followed the merman into the dark.

Once again patches of violet light glimmered over their heads as the passage narrowed and sloped downward. Dalgard tried to remember the general geography of the section which was above them now. He had assumed that this way with its dank chill must give on the river. But when they had pattered on for a long distance, he knew that either they had passed beneath the stream or that he was totally lost as to direction.

As their eyes adjusted to the gloom of the passage the violet light grew stronger. So Dalgard saw clearly when Sssuri whirled and faced back along the way they had come, his body in a half crouch, his knife ready in his hand.

Dalgard, his bow useless in the damp, drew his own sword-knife. But, though his mind probed and he listened, he could sense or hear nothing on their trail.

8

AIRLIFT

They were air-borne once more, but Raf was not pleased. In the seat beside him, which Captain Hobart should be occupying, there now squirmed an alien warrior who apparently was uncomfortable in the chair-like depression so different from the low stools he was accustomed to. Soriki was still in the second passenger place, but he, too, shared that with another of the men from the city who rested across bony knees a strange weapon rather like a Terran rifle.

No, the spacemen were not prisoners. According to the official statement they were allies. But, Raf wondered, as against his will he followed the globe in a northeastern course, how long would that fiction last if they refused to fall in with any suggestions the aliens might make? He did not doubt that there was on board the globe some surprise which could shoot the flitter out of the air, if, for example, he adjusted the controls before him and bore west toward the mountains and the safety of the space ship. Either of the aliens he now transported could bring him under control by using those weapons, which might do anything from boiling a man in some unknown ray to smothering him in gas. He had not seen the arms in action, and he did not want to.

Yet Hobart and Lablet did not, as far as he could tell, share his suspicions. Lablet was eager to see the mysterious storehouse, and the captain was either moved by the same desire or else had long since deduced the folly of trying to make a break for it Thus they were now heading seaward with the captain and Lablet sharing quarters with the leaders of the expedition on board the globe, and Raf and the com-tech, with companions—or guards—bringing up the rear. The aliens had even insisted on stripping the flitter of much of its Terran equipment before they left the city, pointing out that the cleared storage space would be filled with salvage when they made the return voyage.

The globe had been trailing along the coastline, and now it angled out to glide over a long finger of cape, rocky and waterworn, which pointed at almost a right angle into the sea. This dwindled into a reef of rock, like the nail on a finger. The sea ahead was no unbroken expanse. Instead there was a series of islands, some merely tops of reefs over which the waves broke, others more substantial, rising well above the threatening water, and one or two showing the green of vegetation.

The chain of islets extended so far out that when the flitter passed over the last one the main continent was out of sight. Now only water stretched beneath them. The globe skidded on as if its pilot had given it an extra burst of power, and Raf accelerated in turn, having no desire to lose his guide. But they were not to make the ocean-wide trip in one jump.

At midday he saw again a break in the smooth carpet of waves, another island, or perhaps the southern tip of a northern continent for the land swept in that direction as far as he could see. The globe spiraled down to make a neat landing on a flat plateau, and Raf prepared to join it. When the undercarriage of the flitter jarred lightly on the rock, he saw signs that this was a man-or alien-fashioned place which must have had much use in the dim past when his new companions ruled all their native world.

The rock had been smoothed off to a flat surface, and at its perimeter were several small domed buildings. Yet, as there had been in the countryside and in the city, except at its very heart, there was an aura of desertion at the site.

Both his alien passengers jumped out of the flitter, as if only too pleased at their release from the Terran flyer. For the first time Raf was shaken out of his own preoccupation with his dislike for the aliens to wonder if they could be moved by a similar distaste for Terrans. Lablet might be interested in that as a scientific problem—the pilot only knew how he felt and that was not comfortable.

Soriki got out and walked across the rock, stretching. But for a long moment Raf remained where he was, behind the controls of the flyer. He was as cramped and tired of travel as the com-tech, perhaps even more so since the responsibility of the flight had been his. And had they landed in open country he would have liked to have thrown himself down on the ground, taking off his helmet and unhooking his tunic collar to let the fresh wind blow through his hair and across his skin. Perhaps that would take away the arid dust of centuries, which, to his mind, had grimed him since their hours in the city. But here was no open country, only a landing space which reminded him too much of the roof of the building in the metropolis.

A half-dozen of the breastplated warriors filed out of the globe and went to the nearest dome, returning with heavy boxes. Fuel—supplies—Raf shrugged off the problem. The pilot was secretly relieved when Captain Hobart dropped out of the hatch in the globe and made his way over to the flitter.

"Everything running smoothly?" he asked with a glance at the two aliens who were Raf's passengers.

"Yes, sir. Any idea how much farther—?" Raf questioned.

Hobart shrugged. "Until we work out basic language difficulties," he muttered, "who knows anything? There is at least one more of these way stations. They don't run on atomics, need some kind of fuel, and they have to have new supplies every so often. Their head man can't understand why it isn't necessary for us to do the same."

"Has he suggested that his techneers want a look at our motors, sir?"

Hobart unbent a little. It was as if in that question he had read something which pleased him. "So far we've managed not to understand that. And if anyone tries it on his own, refer him to me—understand?"

"Yes, sir!" Some of the relief in Raf's tone came through, and he saw that the captain was watching him narrowly.

"You don't like these people, Kurbi?"

The pilot replied with the truth. "I don't feel easy with them, sir. Not that they've shown any unfriendliness. Maybe it's because they're alien—"

He had said the wrong thing and knew it immediately.

"That sounds like prejudice, Kurbi!" Hobart's voice carried the snap of a reprimand.

"Yes, sir," Raf said woodenly. That had done it as far as the captain was concerned. The fierce racial and economical prejudices which had been the keystones of the structure of Pax had left their shadow on Terra's thinking. Nowadays a man would better be condemned for murder than for prejudice against another—it was the unforgivable crime. And in that unconsidered answer Raf had rendered unreliable in the eyes of authority any future report on the aliens which he might be forced to make.

Silently cursing his lack of judgment, Raf made a careful check of the flyer, which might not be necessary but going through the motions of doing his duty gave him some relief. Once the idea struck him of claiming some trouble that would take them back to the spacer for repairs. But Hobart was too good a mechanic himself not to see through that.

They covered the second stage of their flight by evening, this time putting down on an island where, by some ancient and titanic feat of labor, the top had been sheared off a central mountain to make a base. A ring of reefs cut off the land from the action of the waves. At once a party of aliens left the main company and made their way down the mountain to prowl along the shore. They made a discovery of sorts, for Raf saw them ring in some object they had pulled up on the sand. What it was and what meaning it had for them they did not try to explain to the Terrans.

The party spent the night there, the four spacemen wrapped in their sleeping rolls by the flitter, the aliens in their globe ship. The Terrans did not miss the fact that the others had unobtrusively posted guards at the only two places where the mountain could be climbed. And each of those guards cradled in the crook of his arm one of the rifle weapons.

They were aroused shortly after dawn. As far as Raf could see the island was barren of life, or else any creature native to it kept prudently out of the way while the flyers were there. They took off, the globe rising like a balloon into the morning sky, the flitter waiting until it was air-borne before scaling after it.

The mountainous island where they had based was the sea sentinel of an archipelago, which they saw spread out below them as if someone had flung a handful of pebbles into a shallow pool. Most of the islands were merely rocky crags. But there were two which showed the green of small open fields, and Raf thought he caught a glimpse of a dome house on the last.

They were now over a region thick with islands, the first collection giving way to a second and then a third. Raf, expecting no sudden move on the part of the globe he trailed, was startled when the alien ship made a downward swoop. At the same time the warrior seated beside him tugged at the sleeve of his tunic and jabbed a finger toward the ground, clearly an order to follow. Raf cut speed and cautiously lost altitude, determined that he was not going to be rushed into any move for which he did not know the reason.

The globe was hovering over a small island set a little apart from the others. A moment later Soriki's excited voice drew Raf's attention from his controls to what was going on below.

"There's, people down there! Look at them run!"

They were too far away to be sure of the nature of the brown-gray things so close to the color of the sea-washed rock that they could only be detected when they moved. But it was evident that they were alive, and as Raf brought the flitter closer, he was also certain that they ran on their two hind feet instead of on an animal's four pads.

From the under part of the globe ship licked a tongue of fire.

With the force of a whiplash it coursed across the rock and in its passing embrace, the creatures below writhed and withered to charred heaps. They had no chance under that methodical blasting. The alien beside Raf signaled again for a drop. He patted the weapon that he held and motioned for Raf to release the covering of the windshield. But the pilot shook his head firmly.

This might be war. The aliens could have a very good reason for their deadly attack on the creatures surprised below. But he wanted no part of it, nor did he want to get any closer to the scene of slaughter. And he made an emphatic gesture that the windshield could not be opened while the flitter was airborne.

But as he did so they glided down, and he caught a single good look at what was going on on the rock—a look which remained to haunt his dreams for long years to come. For now he saw clearly the creatures who ran fruitlessly for safety. Some reached the edge of the cliff and leaped to what was an easier death in the sea. But too many others could not make it and died in flaming agony. And they were not all of one size!

Children! There was no mistaking the infant in its mother's arms, the two small ones who fled hand in hand until one stumbled and the burning lash caught them both as the other strove to pull the fallen to its feet. Raf gagged. He triggered the controls and soared up and away, fighting the heaving in his middle, shaking off with one savage jerk the insistent pawing hand of the alien who wanted to join in the fun.

"Did you see that?" he demanded of Soriki.

For once the com-tech sounded subdued. "Yes," he replied shortly.

"Those were children," Raf hammered home the point.

"Young ones anyway," the com-tech conceded. "Maybe they aren't people. They had fur all over them—"

Raf grinned mirthlessly. Should he now accuse Soriki of prejudice? What did it matter if a thinking creature was clothed in a space suit, silken bandages, or natural fur—it was still a thinking creature. And he was sure that those had been intelligent creatures he had just seen blasted without a chance to fight back. If these were the enemy the aliens feared, he could understand the vicious cruelty of the attack which had killed the man he had been shown back in the city. Fire against primitive spears was not equal, and when the spears got their chance they must make up for much to balance the scales of justice.

He did not even wonder why his emotions were so wholeheartedly enlisted upon the side of the furred people. Nor did he try to analyze his feelings. He was only sure that more than ever he wanted to be free of the aliens and out of this whole venture.

The warrior sharing his seat was sulking now, twisting about to look back at the island as Raf circled in ever-widening glides to get away from the site and yet not lose track of the globe when it would have finished its dirty business and take once more to the air. But the alien ship was in no hurry to leave.

"They are making sure," Soriki reported. "Giving the whole island a fire bath. I wonder what that stuff is—"

"I'd just as soon not know," Raf returned from between set teeth. "If that is one of their pieces of precious knowledge, we're as well off without it—" he stopped short. Perhaps he had said too much. But Terra had been racked by the torrid horror of atomic war, until all his kind had been so revolted that it was bred into them not to meddle again with such weapons. And war by fire aroused in them that old horror. Surely Soriki must feel it too, and when the com-tech did not comment, Raf was sure of that. He hoped that the slaughter had made some impression on the captain and on Lablet into the bargain.

But when, as if sated with killing, the globe rose again from its position over the island, moving almost sluggishly into the fresh sky, he had to follow it on. More islands were below, and he feared that each one might show some sign of life and tempt the killers to a second hunting.

Luckily that did not happen. The chains of islands became a cape as they had on the coast of the western continent. And now the globe swung to the south, trailing the shore line. Forests made green splotches with bluish overtones running from the sea cliffs back to carpet the land. So far no signs of civilization were to be seen. This land was as untouched as that where the spacer had landed.

Then they saw the bay, stretching out wide arms to engulf the sea. It could have harbored a whole fleet. And marching down to its waters were broad levels of buildings, a giant's staircase leading from sea to cliff tops.

"They had it here—!"

Raf saw what Soriki meant by that outburst. Destruction had struck. He had seen the atomic ruins of his own world, those which were free enough from radiation to explore. But he had never seen anything like these chilling scars. In long strips the very stone which provided foundation for the tiered city had been churned and boiled, had run in rivulets of lava down to the sea, enclosing narrow tongues of still untouched structures. The fire whip the globe had used, magnified to some infinitely greater extent—? It could be.

The alien at his side pressed tightly against the windshield gazing down at the ruins. And now he mouthed a gabble of words which was echoed by his fellow sitting with Soriki. Their excitement must mean that this was their goal. Raf slacked speed, waiting for the globe to point a way to a landing.

But to his surprise the alien ship shot forward inland. The long day was almost over as they came to a second city with a river knotting a ribbon through its middle. Here were no traces of the fury which had laded the seaport with havoc. This collection of buildings seemed whole and perfect.

There was, oddly enough, no landing strip within the city. The globe coasted over the rough oval and came down in open fields to the west. It was a maneuver which Raf copied, though he first dropped a flare as a precaution and brought the flier down in its red glare, with the warrior expressing shrill disapproval.

"I don't think they like fireworks," Soriki remarked.

Raf snorted. "So they don't like fireworks! Well, I don't like crack-ups, and I'm the pilot!" But he didn't believe that the com-tech was really protesting. Soriki had been very quiet since they had witnessed the attack on the island.

"Grim-looking place," was his second comment as they touched ground.

Since Raf privately had held that opinion of all the alien settlements he had so far seen, he agreed. Their two alien passengers were out of the flitter as soon as he opened the bubble shield. And as they stood by the Terran flyer, they held their weapons ready, facing out into the dusk as if they half expected trouble. After the earlier episode that day, Raf did not wonder at their preparedness. Terror begets terror, and ruthlessness arouses retaliation in kind.

"Kurbi! Soriki!" Hobart's voice sounded out of the shadows. "Stay where you are for the present."

Soriki settled deeper in his seat. "He doesn't have to tell me to brake jets," he muttered. "I like it here—"

Raf did not need to echo that. He had a strong surmise that had he been tempted to roam away from the flitter the move would not have been encouraged by the alien guardsmen. If this was their treasure city, they would not welcome any independent investigation by strangers.

When the captain joined them, he was accompanied by the officer who had first shown Raf the globe. And the warrior was either disturbed or angry, for he was talking in a steady stream and his hands were whirling in explanatory gestures.

"They didn't like that flare," Hobart remarked. But there was no reproof in his words. As a spacer pilot he knew that Raf had only done what duty demanded. "We're to remain here— for the night."

"Where's Lablet?" Soriki wanted to know.

"He's staying with Yussoz, the alien commander. He thinks he has the language problem about solved."

"Good enough." Soriki pulled out his bed roll. "We're out of touch with the ship—"

There was a second of silence, unduly prolonged it seemed to Raf. Then Hobart spoke:

"We couldn't expect to keep in call forever. The best com has its range. When did you lose contact?"

"Just before these wrapped-up heroes played with fire back there. I gave the boys all I knew up until then. They know we were headed west, and they had us beamed as long as they could."

So it wasn't too bad, thought Raf. But he didn't like it, even with that mitigating factor. To all purposes the four Terrans were now surrounded by some twenty times their number, in an unknown country, out of all communication with the rest of their kind. It could add up to disaster.

9

SEA GATE

"What is it?" Dalgard asked his question as Sssuri, his attention still on their back trail, stole along cautiously on a retracing of their path.

But that retreat ended abruptly with the merman plastered against the wall, his whole shadowy form a tense warning which stopped Dalgard short. In that moment the answer flashed from mind to mind.

"There are those which follow—"

"Snake-devils? Those Others?" The colony scout supplied the only two explanations he had, sending his own thought out questing. But as usual he could not hope to equal the more sensitive merman whose race had always used that form of communication.

"Those who have long haunted the darkness," was the only reply he could get.

But Sssuri's actions were far more indicative of danger. For the merman turned and caught at Dalgard, pulling the larger colonist along a step or two with the urgency of his grip.

"We cannot return this way—and we must travel fast!"

For Sssuri who would face and had faced up to a snake-devil with a spear his sole weapon, this timidity was new. Dalgard was wise enough to accept his verdict of the wisdom of flight. Together they ran along the underground corridor, soon putting a mile between them and the point where the merman had first taken alarm.

"From what do we flee?" As the merman began to slacken pace, Dalgard sent that query.

"There are those who live in this darkness. By one, or by two, we could speedily remove them from life. But they hunt in packs and they are as greedy for the kill as are the snake-devils scenting meat. Also they are intelligent. Once, long before the days of burning, they served Those Others as hunters of game. And Those Others tried to make them ever more intelligent and crafty so they might be sent to hunt without a huntsman. At last they grew too knowing for their masters. Then Those Others, realizing their menace, tried to kill them all with traps and tricks. But only the most stupid and the slowest were so disposed of. The others withdrew into underground ways such as this, venturing forth only in the dark of night."

"But if they are intelligent," countered the scout, "why can they not be reached by the mind touch?"

"Through the years they have developed their own ways of thought. And these are not the simple creatures of the sun, or such as the runners. Once they were taught to answer only to Those Others. Now they answer only to each other. But"—he spread out his hands in one of his quick, nervous gestures— "to those who are cornered by one of their packs, they are sudden death!"

Since they could not, by Sssuri's reckoning, turn back, there was only one course before them, to follow the passage they had chanced upon. The merman was certain that it underran the river and that eventually they would reach the sea—unless some side turn before that point would make them free in the countryside once more.

Dalgard doubted if it had ever been a well-used way. And the presence of earth falls here and there, over which they stumbled and clawed their way, led him to consider the wisdom of keeping on to what might be a dead end. But his trust in Sssuri's judgment was great, and as the merman plowed forward with every appearance of confidence, he continued to trot along without complaint.

They snatched moments of rest, taking turns at guard. But the walls about them were so unchanging that it was hard to measure time or distance. Dalgard chewed at his emergency rations, a block of dried meat and fruit pounded together to an almost rocklike consistency, and tried to make the crumbs he sucked loose satisfy his growing hunger.

The passageway was growing damper; water trickled down the walls and gathered in fetid pools on the floor. Dalgard's dislike of the place grew. His shoulders hunched involuntarily as he strode along, for his imagination pictured the rock above them giving away to dump tons of the oily river water down to engulf them. But though Sssuri avoided splashing through the pools wherever he might, he did not appear to find anything upsetting about the moisture.

At last the human could stand it no longer. "How much farther to the sea?" he asked without any hope of a real answer.

As he had expected him to do, Sssuri shrugged. "We should

be close. But having never trod this way before, how can I tell you?"

Once more they rested, choosing a stretch which was reasonably dry, munching their dried food and drinking sparingly from the stoppered duocorn horns which swung from their belts. A man would have to be dying of thirst, Dalgard thought, before he would palm up any of the stagnant water from the passage pools.

He drifted off into a troubled sleep in which he fled beneath a sky which was a giant lid in the hand of an unseen enemy, a lid which was slowly lowered to crush him flat. He awoke with a start to find Sssuri's cool, scaled fingers stroking his shoulder.

"Dream demons walk these roads." The words drifted into his half-awake mind.

"They do indeed," he roused to answer.

"It is always so where Those Others have been. They leave behind them the thoughts which breed such dreams to trouble the sleep of those who are not of their kind. Let us go. I would like to be out of this place under the clean sky, where no ancient wickedness hangs to poison the air and thought."

Either the merman had miscalculated the direction of their route or the river mouth was much farther from the inland city than they had believed, for, though they pushed on for what seemed like weary hours, they came to no upward slope, no exit to the world they knew.

Instead Dalgard began to realize that just the opposite was true. At last he could stand it no longer and broke out with what he feared, hoping that Sssuri would deny that fear.

"We are going downhill!"

To his disappointment the merman agreed. "It has been so for the last thousand of our paces. It is my belief that this leads not to the sun but out under the sea."

Dalgard missed a step. To Sssuri the sea was home and perhaps the thought of being under its floor was not disturbing. The land-born human was not so prepared. If he had experienced discomfort under the river, what would it be like under the ocean? His terrifying dream of a lid being pressed down upon him flashed back into his mind. But his companion was continuing:

"There will be doors, perhaps into the sea itself."

"For you," Dalgard pointed out, "but I am no dweller in the depths."

"Neither were Those Others, yet they used these ways. And I tell you"—in his earnestness the merman laid his hand once more on Dalgard's arm—"to turn back now is out of the question. The death which haunts the darkness is still sniffing out our trail."

Dalgard glanced involuntarily over his shoulder. By the faint and limited light of the purple disks he could see little or nothing. An army might creep there undetected.

"But—" His protest was in answer to the merman's seeming unconcern.

Sssuri at the first intimation that the hunters were behind them had shown wariness. Now he did not appear to care.

"They had fed," he replied. "Scouts follow because we are something new and thus suspect. When hunger rises once more in them, and their scouts report that we are meat, then is the time to draw knives and prepare for battle. But before that hour we may have won free. Let us search for the gate we now need."

However confident the merman might be, Dalgard could not match that confidence. In the open air he would have faced a snake-devil four times his size without any more emotion than a hunter's instinctive caution. But here in the dark, unable to rid himself of the belief that thousands of tons of sea water hung over his head, he found himself starting at any sound, his knife bare and ready in his sweating hand.

He noted that Sssuri had stepped up the pace, passing into his sure-footed glide which made Dalgard exert himself to keep up. Before them the corridor stretched without a break. The merman's promised exit, if it existed, was still out of sight.

It was difficult to gauge time in this dark hall, but Dalgard thought that they were at least an hour farther on their way when Sssuri paused abruptly once more, his head cocked in a listening attitude, as if he caught some whisper of sound too rarefied for his human companion.

"Now—" the thought hissed as if he spat the words, "they hunger—and they hunt!"

He bounded forward with a spurt, which Dalgard copied, and they ran lightly, the dust undisturbed in years puffing up beneath the merman's bare, scaled feet and Dalgard's hide boots. Still the unbroken walls, the feeble patches of violet in the ceiling. But no exit. And what good would any exit do him, Dalgard thought, if it opened under the sea?

"There are islands off the coast—many islands—" Sssuri caught him up. "It is in my mind that we shall find our door on one of those. But—run now, knife brother, for those at our heels awake and thirst for flesh and blood. They have decided that we are not to be feared but may be run down for their pleasure."

Dalgard weighed his knife in his hand. "They shall find us with fangs," he promised grimly.

"It will be better if they do not find us at all," returned Sssuri.

A burning arch of pain encased Dalgard's lower ribs, and his breath came in gusts of hastily sucked air as their flight kept on, down the endless corridor. Sssuri was also showing signs of the grueling pace, his round head bent forward, his furred legs pumping as if only his iron will kept them moving. And the determination which kept him going was communicated to the scout as a graver warning than any thought message of fear.

They were passing under one of the infrequent violet lights when Dalgard got something else—a mental thrust so quick and sharp it was as if a sword had cut through the daze of fatigue to reach his brain. Yet that had not come from Sssuri, for it was totally alien, wavering on a band so near the extreme edge of his consciousness that it pricked, receded, and pricked again as a needle might.

This was no message of fear or warning, but of implacable stubbornness and ravening hunger. And in that instant Dalgard knew that it came from what was sniffing out their trail, and he no longer wondered that the hunters were immune to other mental contact. One could not reason with—that!

He spurted forward, matching the merman's acceleration of speed. But to Dalgard's horror he saw that his companion now ran with one hand brushing along the wall, as if he needed that support.

"Sssuri!"

His thought met a wall of concentration through which he could not break. In a way he was reassured—for a moment, until another of those stabs from their pursuers struck him. He longed to look back, to see what hunted them. But he dared not break stride to do that.

"Ahhhh!" The welcoming cry from Sssuri brought his attention back to his companion as the merman broke into a wild run.

Dalgard summoned up his last rags of energy and coursed after him. Sssuri had halted before a dark lump which protruded from the side of the corridor.

"A sea lock!" Sssuri's claws were clicking over the surface of the hatch, seeking the secret of its latch.

Panting, Dalgard leaned against the opposite wall. Just as a protest formed in his mind he heard something else, the pad of feet, many feet, echoing down the corridor. And somehow he was able now to look.

Round spots of light, dull, greenish, close to the ground, as if someone had flung a handful of phosphorescence into the dark. But this was no phosphorescence! Eyes! Eyes—he tried to count and knew it was impossible to so reckon the number of the pack that ran mute but ready. Nor could he distinguish more than a very shadowy glimpse of forms which glided close to the ground with an unpleasant sinuosity.

"Ahhhhh!" Again Sssuri's paean of triumph.

There was the grate of unwilling metal forced to move, a puff of air redolent with the sea striking their bodies in chill threat, the brightness of violet light stepped up to a point far beyond the lamps in the corridor.

With it came no rush of drowning water as Dalgard had half expected, and when the merman clambered through the hatch he prepared to follow, well aware that the eyes, and the pattering feet which bore them, were now almost within range.

There was a snarl from the passage, and a black thing sprang at the scout. Without clear sight of what he was fighting, he struck down with his knife and felt it slit flesh. The snarl was a scream of rage as the creature twisted in midair for a second try at him. In that instant Sssuri, leaning halfway out of the hatch, struck in his turn, thrusting his bone knife into shadows which now boiled with life.

Dalgard leaped for the lock door, kicking out swiftly and feeling the toe of his boot contact with a crunch against one of those darting shades, sending it back end over end into the press where its fellows turned snapping upon it. Then Sssuri grabbed at him, bringing him in, and together they slammed the hatch, feeling it shake with the shock of thudding bodies as the pack outside went mad in their frustration.

While the merman fastened the locking bar, bringing out of the long-motionless metal another protesting screech, Dalgard had a chance to look about him. They were in a room some eight or nine feet long, the violet light showing up well tangles of equipment hanging from pegs on the walls, a pile of small cylinders on the floor. At the far end of the chamber was another hatch door, locked with the same type of bar as Sssuri had just lowered to seal the inner one. The merman nodded to it.

"The sea—"

Dalgard slid his knife back into its sheath. So the sea lay beyond. He did not welcome the thought of passing through that door. Like all of his race he could swim—perhaps his feats in the water would have astonished the men of the planet from which his tribe had emigrated. But unlike the mermen, he was not sea-born, nor equipped by nature with a secondary breathing apparatus to make him as free in the world of water as he was on land. Sssuri might crawl through that hatch without fear. For Dalgard it was as big a test as to turn and face what now raged in the corridor on the inner side.

"There is no hope that they will go now," Sssuri answered his vague question. "They are stubborn. And hours—or even days—will mean nothing. Also they can leave a guard there and rove at will, to return upon signal. That is their way."

This left only the sea door. Sssuri padded across the chamber and reached up to free one of the strange objects dangling from the wall pegs. Like all things made of the marvelous substance used by Those Others for any article which might be exposed to the elements, it seemed as perfect as on the day it had first been hung there, though that date might be a hundred or more Astran years earlier. The merman uncoiled a length of thin, flexible piping which joined a two-foot canister with a flat piece of metallic fabric.

"Those Others could not breathe under the water, as you cannot," he explained as he worked deftly and swiftly. "Within my own memory we have trapped their scouts wearing aids such as these so that they might spy upon our safe places. But their last foray was some years ago and at that time we taught them such a lesson that they have not dared to return. Since they are not unlike you in body and since you breathe the same air aboveground, there is no reason why this should not take you out of here."

Dalgard accepted the apparatus. A couple of elastic metal bands fastened the canister to the chest of the wearer. The fabric molded into a perfect, tight face mask as it touched the skin.

Sssuri went to the pile of cylinders. Choosing one he tinkered with its pointed cone, to be rewarded with a thin hiss.

"Ahhhh—" again his recognition of the rightness of things. "These still contain air." He tested two more and then brought all three back to where Dalgard stood, the canister strapped into place, the mask ready in his hand. With infinite care the merman fitted two of the cylinders into the canister and then was forced to set the other aside.

"We could not change them while under water anyway," he explained. "So it will do little good to take extra supplies with us."

Trying not to speculate on the amount of air he could carry in the cylinders, Dalgard fastened on the mask, adjusted the air tube, and sucked. Air flowed—he could breathe! Only— for how long?

Sssuri, seeing that his companion was fully provided for, worked at the bar locking the sea hatch. But in the end it took their combined strength to spring that barrier and win through to a small cubby which was the actual sea lock.

Dalgard knew one moment of resistance as the merman closed the hatch behind them. For an instant it seemed that the dubious safety of the dressing chamber and a faint hope of the hunters' giving up their vigil was better than what might lie before them now. But Sssuri pushed shut the hatch, and Dalgard stood quietly, without offering any visible protest.

He tried to draw even breaths—slowly—as the merman activated the lock. When the water curled in from hidden openings, rising from ankle to calf and then to knee, its chill striking through flesh to bone, he kept to the same stolid waiting, though this seemed almost worse than a sudden gush of water sweeping them out in its embrace.

The liquid swirled about Dalgard's waist now, tugging at his belt, his arrow quiver, tapping on the bottom of the canister which held his precious air supply. His brow, shielded from the wet by its casing, was swallowed up inch by inch.

As the water lapped at his chin, the outer door opened with a slow inward push which suggested that the machinery controlling it had grown sluggish with the years. Sssuri, perfectly at home, darted out as soon as the opening was large enough to afford him an exit. And his thought came back to reassure the more clumsy landsman.

"We are in the shallows—land rises ahead. The roots of an island. There is nothing to fear—" The word ended abruptly in what was like a mental gasp of either astonishment or fear.

Knowing all the menaces which might lie in wait, even in the shallows of the sea, Dalgard drew his knife once more as he plowed through water—ready to rescue or at least to offer what aid he could.

10

THE DEAD GUARDIANS

The spacemen spent a cramped and almost sleepless night. Although in his training on Terra, on his trial trips to Mars and the harsh Lunar valleys, Raf had known weird surroundings and climates, inimical to his kind, he had always been able to rest almost by the exercise of his will. But now, curled in his roll, he was alert to every sound out of the moonless night, finding himself listening—for what he did not know.

Though there were sounds in plenty. The whistling call of some night bird, the distant lap, lap of water which he associated with the river curving through the long-deserted city, the rustle of grass as either the wind or some passing animal disturbed it.

"Not the best place in the world for a nap," Soriki observed out of the dark as Raf wriggled, trying to find a more comfortable position. "I'll be glad to see these bandaged boys on the ground waving good-bye as we head away from them—fast—"

"Those weren't animals they killed—back on that island." Raf brought out what was at the heart of his trouble.

"They wore fur instead of clothing." Soriki's reply was delivered in a colorless, even voice. "We have apes on Terra, but they are not men."

Raf stared up at the sky in which stars were sprinkled like carelessly flung dust motes. "What is a 'man'?" he returned, repeating the classical question which was a debating point in all the space training centers.

For so long his kind had wondered that. Was a "man" a biped with certain easily recognized physical characteristics? Well, by that ruling the furry things which had fled fruitlessly from the flames of the globe might well qualify. Or was "man" a certain level of intelligence, no matter what form housed that intelligence? They were supposed to accept the latter definition. Though, in spite of the horror of prejudice, Raf could not help but believe that too many Terrans secretly thought of "man" only as a creature in their own general image. By that prejudiced rule it was correct to accept the aliens as "men" with whom they could ally themselves, to condemn the furry people because they were not smooth-skinned, did not wear clothing, nor ride in mechanical transportation.

Yet somewhere within Raf at that moment was the nagging feeling that this was all utterly wrong, that the Terrans had not made the right choice. And that now "men" were *not* standing together. But he had no intention of spilling that out to Soriki.

"Man is intelligence." The com-tech was answering the question Raf had almost forgotten that he had asked the moment before. Yes, the proper conventional reply. Soriki was not going to be caught out with any claim of prejudice.

Odd—when Pax had ruled, there were thought police and the

cardinal sin was to be a liberal, to experiment, to seek knowledge. Now the wheel had turned—to be conservative was suspect. To suggest that some old ways were better was to exhibit the evil signs of prejudice. Raf grinned wryly. Sure, he had wanted to reach the stars, had fought doggedly to come to the very spot where he now was. So why was he tormented now with all these second thoughts? Why did he feel every day less akin to the men with whom he had shared the voyage? He had had wit enough to keep his semirebellion under cover, but since he had taken the flitter into the morning sky above the landing place of the spacer, that task of self-discipline was becoming more and more difficult.

"Did you notice," the com-tech said, going off on a new track, "that these painted boys were not too quick about blasting along to their strongbox? I'd say that they thought some bright rocket jockey might have rigged a surprise for them somewhere in there—"

Now that Soriki mentioned it, Raf remembered that the alien party who had gone into the city had huddled together, and that several of the black-and-white warriors had fanned out ahead as scouts might in enemy territory.

"They didn't go any farther than that building to the west either."

That Raf had not noticed, but he was willing to accept Soriki's observation. The com-tech had a ready eye for details. He'd better pay closer attention himself. This was no time to explore the why and wherefore of his present position. So, if they went no farther than that building, it would argue that the aliens themselves didn't care to go about here after nightfall. For he was certain that the isolated structure Soriki had pointed out was not the treasure house they had come to loot.

The night wore on and sometime during it Raf fell asleep. But the two or three hours of restless, dream-filled unconsciousness was not what he needed, and he blinked in the dawn with eyes which felt as if they were filled with hot sand. In the first gray light a covey of winged things, which might or might not have been birds, arose from some roosting place within the city, wheeled three times over the building, and then vanished out over the countryside.

Raf pulled himself out of his roll, made a sketchy toilet with the preparations in a belt kit, and looked about with little favor for either the scene or his part in it. The globe, sealed as if ready for a take-off, was some distance away, but installed about halfway between it and the flitter were two of the alien warriors. Perhaps they had changed watches during the night. If they had not, they could go without sleep to an amazing degree, for as Raf walked in a circle about the flyer to limber up, they watched him closely, nor did their grips on their odd weapons loosen. And he had a very clear idea that if he stepped over some invisible boundary he would be in for trouble.

When he came back to the flitter, Soriki was awake and stretching.

"Another day," the com-tech drawled. "And I could do with something besides field rations." He made a face at the small tin of concentrates he had dug out of the supply compartment.

"We'd do well to be headed west," Raf ventured.

"Now you can come in with that on the com again!" Soriki answered with unwonted emphasis. "The sooner I see the old girl standing on her pins in the middle distance, the better I'll feel. You know"—he looked up from his preoccupation with the ration package and gazed out over the city—"this place gives me the shivers. That other town was bad enough. But at least there were people living there. Here's nothing at all— at least nothing I want to see."

"What about all the wonders they've promised to show us?" countered Raf.

Soriki grinned. "And how much do we understand of their mouth-and-hand talk? Maybe they were promising us wonders, maybe they were offering to take us to where we could have our throats cut more conveniently—for them! I tell you, if I go for a walk with any of these painted faces, I'm going to have at least three of my fingers resting on the grip of my stun gun. And I'd advise you to do the same—if I didn't know that you were already watching these blast-happy harpies out of the corner of your eye. Ha—company. Oh, it's the captain—"

The hatch of the globe had opened, and a small party was descending the ladder, conspicuous among them the form and uniform of Captain Hobart. The aliens remained in a cluster at the foot of the ladder while the Terran commander crossed to the flitter.

"You"—he pointed to Raf—"are to come along with us."

"Why, sir?" "What about me, sir?" The questions from the two at the flitter came together.

"I said that one of you had to remain by the machine. Then they said that you, in particular, must come along, Kurbi."

"But I'm the pilot—" Raf began and then realized that it was just that fact which had made the aliens attach him to the exploring party. If they believed that the Terran flitter was immobilized when he, and he alone, was not behind its controls, this was just the move they would make. But there they were wrong. Soriki might not be able to repair or service the motor, but in a pinch he could take it up, send it westward, and land it beside the spacer. Each and every man aboard the *RS 10* had that much training.

Now the com-tech was scowling. He had grasped the significance of that arrangement as quickly as Raf. "How long do I wait for you, sir?" he asked in a voice which had lost its usual good-humored drawl.

And at that inquiry Captain Hobart showed signs of irritation. "Your suspicions are not founded on facts," he stated firmly. "These people have displayed no signs of wanting to harm us. And an attitude of distrust at this point might be fatal for future friendly contact. Lablet is sure that they have a highly complex society, probably advanced beyond Terran standards, and that their technical skills will be of vast benefit to us. As it happens we have come at just the right moment in their history, when they are striving to get back on their feet after a disastrous series of wars. It is as if a group of off-world explorers had allied themselves with us after the Burn-Off. We can exchange information which will be of mutual benefit."

"If any off-world explorers had set down on Terra after the Burn-Off," observed Soriki softly, "they would have come up against Pax. And just how long would they have lasted?"

Hobart had turned away. If he heard that half-whisper, he did not choose to acknowledge it. But the truth in the com-tech's words made an impression on Raf, a crew of aliens who had been misguided enough to seek out and try to establish friendly relations with the officials of Pax would have had a short and most unhappy shrift. If all the accounts of that dark dictatorship were true, they would have vanished from Terra, and not in their ships either. What if something like Pax ruled here? They had no way of knowing for sure.

Raf's eyes met Soriki's, and the com-tech's hand dropped to hook fingers in his belt within touching distance of his side arm. The flitter pilot nodded.

"Kurbi!" Hobart's impatient call sent him on his way. But there was some measure of relief in knowing that Soriki was left behind and that they had this slender link with escape.

He had tramped the streets of that other alien city. There there had been some semblance of habitation; here was abandonment. Earth drifted in dunes to half block the lanes, and here and there climbing vines had broken down masonry and had dislodged blocks of the paved sideways and courtyards.

The party threaded their way from one narrow lane to another, seeming to avoid the wider open stretches of the principal thoroughfares, Raf became aware of an unpleasant odor in the air which he vaguely associated with water, and a few minutes afterward he caught glimpses of the river between the buildings which fronted on it. Here the party turned abruptly at a right angle, heading westward once more, passing vast, blank-walled structures which might have been warehouses.

One of the aliens just ahead of Raf in the line of march suddenly swung around, his weapon pointing up, and from its nose shot a beam of red-yellow light which brought an answering shrill scream as a large, winged creature came fluttering down. The killer kicked at the crumpled thing as he passed. As far as Raf could see there had been no reason for that wanton slaying.

The head of the party had reached a doorway, sealed shut by what looked like a solid slab of material. He placed both palms flat down on its surface at shoulder height and leaned forward against it, almost as if he were whispering some secret formula. Raf watched the muscles stand up on his slender arms as he exerted strength. And then the door split in two, and his fellows helped him push the separate halves back into the wall.

Lablet, Hobart, and Raf were among the last to enter. It was as if their companions had now forgotten them, for the aliens were pushing on at a pace which took them down an empty corridor at a quickening trot.

The corridor ended in a ramp which did not slope in one straight reach but curled around itself, so that in some places only the presence of a handrail, to which they all clung, kept them from losing balance. Then they gathered in a vaulted room, one of which opened a complete circle of closed doors.

There was some argument among the aliens, a dispute of sorts over which of those doors was to be opened first, and the Terrans drew a little apart, unable to follow the twittering words and lightning-swift gestures.

Raf tried to work out the patterns of color which swirled and looped over each door and around the walls, only to discover that too long an examination of any one band, or an attempt to trace its beginning or end, awoke a sick sensation which approached inner turmoil the longer he looked. At last he had to rest his eyes by studying the gray flooring under his boots.

The aliens finally made up their minds, or else one group was able to outargue the other, for they converged upon a door directly opposite the ramp. Once more they went through the process of unsealing the panels, while the Terrans, drawn by curiosity, were close behind them as they entered the long room beyond. Here were shelves in solid tiers along the walls, crowded with such an array of strange objects that Raf, after one mystified look, thought that it might well take months to sort them all out.

In addition, long tables divided the chamber into aisles. Halfway down one of these narrow passageways the aliens had gathered in a group as silent and intent now as they had been noisy outside. Raf could see nothing to so rivet their attention but a series of scuffed marks in the dust which covered the floor. But an alien, whom he recognized as the officer who had taken him to inspect the globe, moved carefully along that trail, following it to a second door. And as Raf pushed down another aisle, paralleling his course, he was conscious of a sickly sweet, stomach-churning stench. Something was very, very dead and not too far away.

The officer must have come to the same conclusion, for he hurried to open the other door. Before them now was a narrow hall broken by slit windows, near the roof, through which entered sunlight. And one such beam fully illuminated a carcass as large as that of a small elephant, or so it seemed to Raf's startled gaze.

It was difficult to make out the true appearance of the creature, though guessing from the scaled strips of skin it had been reptilian, for the body had been found by scavengers and feasting had been in progress.

The alien officer skirted the corpse gingerly. Raf though that he would like to investigate the body closely but could not force himself to that highly disagreeable task. There was a chorus of excited exclamation from the doorway as others crowded there.

But the officer, having circled the carcass, turned his attention to the dusty floor again. If there had been any trail there, it was now muddled past their reading, for remnants of the grisly meal had been dragged back and forth. The alien picked his way fastidiously through the noxious debris to the end of the long room. Raf, with the same care, toured the edge of the chamber in his wake.

They were out in a smaller passageway, which was taking them underground, the Terran estimated. Then there was a large space with barred cells about it and a second corridor. The stench of the death chamber either clung to them, or was wafted from another point, and Raf gagged as an especially foul blast caught him full in the face. He kept a sharp look about him for signs of those feasters. The feast had not been finished—it might have been that their entrance into the storeroom had disturbed the scavengers. And things formidable enough to drag down that scaled horror were not foes he would choose to meet in these unlighted ways.

The passage began to slope upward once more, and Raf saw a half-moon of light ahead, brilliant light which could only come from the sun. The alien was outlined there as he went out; then he himself was scuffing through sand close upon another death scene. The dead monster had had its counterparts, and here they were, sprawled out, mangled, and torn. Raf remained by the archway, for even the open air and the morning winds could not destroy the reek which seemed as deadly as a gas attack.

It must have disturbed the officer too, for he hesitated. Then with visible effort he advanced toward the hunks of flesh, casting back and forth as if to find some clue to the manner of their death. He was still so engaged when a second alien burst out of the archway, a splintered length of white held out before him as if he had made some important discovery.

The officer grabbed that shaft away from him, turning it around in his hands. And though expression was hard to read on those thin features under the masking face paint, the emotion his whole attitude expressed was surprise tinged with unbelief—as if the object his subordinate had brought was the last he expected to find in that place.

Raf longed to inspect it, but both aliens brushed by him and pattered back down the corridor, the discoverer pouring forth a volume of words to which the officer listened with great intentness. And the Terran pilot had to hurry to keep up with them.

Something he had seen just before he had left the arena remained in his mind: a forearm flung out from the supine body of what appeared to be the largest of the dead things—and on that forearm a bracelet of metal. Were those things pets! Watchdogs? Surely they were not intelligent beings able to forge and wear such ornaments of their own accord. And if they were watchdogs—whom did they serve? He was inclined to believe that the aliens must be their masters, that the monsters had been guardians of the treasure, perhaps. But dead guardians suggested a rifled treasure house. Who and what—?

His mind filled with speculations and questions, Raf trotted behind the others back to the chamber where they had found the first reptile. The alien who had brought the discovery to his commander stepped gingerly through the litter and laid the white rod in a special spot, apparently the place where it had been found.

At a barked order from the officer, two of the others came forward and tugged at the creature's mangled head, which had been freed from the serpent neck, rolling it over to expose the underparts. There was a broad tear there in the flesh, but Raf could see little difference between it and those left by the feasters. However the officer, holding a strip of cloth over his nose, bent stiffly above it for a closer look and then made some statement which sent his command into a babbling clamor.

Four of the lower ranks separated from the group and, with their hand weapons at alert, swung into action, retracing the way back toward the arena. It looked to Raf as if they now expected an attack from that direction.

Under a volley of orders the rest went back to the storeroom, and the officer, noting that Raf still lingered, waved him impatiently after them.

Inside the men spread out, going from shelf to table, selecting things with a speed which suggested that they had been rehearsed in this task and had only a limited time in which to accomplish it. Some took piles of boxes or other containers which were so light that they could manage a half-dozen in an armload, while two or three others struggled pantingly to move a single piece of weird machinery from its bed to the wheeled trolley they had brought. There was to be no lingering on this job—that was certain.

11

ESPIONAGE

Intent upon joining Sssuri, Dalgard left the lock, forgetting his earlier unwillingness, stepping from the small chamber down to the sea bottom, or endeavoring to, although instinctively he had begun to swim and so forged ahead at a different rate of speed.

Waving fronds of giant water plants, such as were found only in the coastal shallows, grew forest fashion but did not hide rocks which stretched up in a sharp rise not too far ahead. The scout could not see the merman, but as he held onto one of those fronds he caught the other's summons:

"Here—by the rocks—!"

Pushing his way through the drifting foliage, Dalgard swam ahead to the foot of the rocky escarpment. And there he saw what had so excited his companion.

Sssuri had just driven away an encircling collection of sand-dwelling scavengers, and what he was on his knees studying intently was an almost clean-picked skeleton of one of his own race. But there was something odd—Dalgard brushed aside a tendril of weed which cut his line of vision and so was able to see clearly.

White and clean most of those bones were, but the skull was blackened, and similar charring existed down one arm and shoulder. That merman had not died from any mishap in the sea!

"It is so," Sssuri replied to his thought. "*They* have come once more to give the flaming death—"

Dalgard, startled, looked up that slope which must lead to the island top above the waves.

"Long dead?" he asked tentatively, already guessing what the other's answer would be.

"The pickers move fast," Sssuri indicated the sand dwellers. "Perhaps yesterday, perhaps the day before—but no longer than that."

"And *they* are up there now?"

"Who can tell? However, *they* do not know the sea, nor the islands—"

It was plain that the merman intended to climb to investigate what might be happening above. Dalgard had no choice but to follow. And it was true that the merpeople had no peers or equals when it came to finding their ways about the sea and the coasts. He was confident that Sssuri could get to the island top and discover just what he wished to learn without a single sentry above, if they had stationed sentries, being the wiser. Whether he himself could operate as efficiently was another matter.

In the end they half climbed, half swam upward, detouring

Andre Norton

swiftly once to avoid the darting attack of a rock hornet, harmless as soon as they moved out of the reach of its questing stinger, for it was anchored for its short life to the rough hollow in which it had been hatched.

Dalgard's head broke water as he rolled through the surf onto a scrap of beach in the lee of a row of tooth-pointed outcrops. It was late evening by the light, and he clawed the mask off his face to draw thankful lungfuls of the good outer air. Sssuri, his fur sleeked tight to his body, waded ashore, shook himself free of excess water, and turned immediately to study the wall of the cliff which guarded the interior of the island.

This was one of a chain of such isles, Dalgard noted, now that he had had time to look about him. And with their many-creviced walls they were just the type of habitations which appealed most strongly to the merpeople. Here could be found the dry inner caves with underwater entrances, which they favored for their group homes. And in the sea were kelp beds for harvesting.

The cliffs did not present too much of a climbing problem. Dalgard divested himself of the diving equipment, tucking it into a hollow which he walled up with stones that he thought the waves would not scour out in a hurry. He might need it again. Then, hitching his belt tighter, pressing what water he could out of his clothing, and settling his bow and quiver to the best advantage at his back, he crossed to where Sssuri was already marking claw holds.

"We may be seen—" Dalgard craned his neck, trying to make out details of what might be waiting above.

The merman shook his head with a quick jerk of negation. "*They* are gone. Behind them remains only death—much death—" And the bleakness of his thoughts reached the scout.

Dalgard had known Sssuri since he was a toddler and the other a cub coming to see the wonders of dry land for the first time. Never, during all their years of close association since, had he felt in the other a desolation so great. And to that emotional blast he could make no answer.

In the twilight, with the last red banners across the sky at their back, they made the climb. And it was as if the merman had closed off his mind to his companion. Flesh fingers touched scaled ones as they moved from one hold to the next, but Sssuri might have been half a world away for all the communication between them. Never had Dalgard been so shut out and with that his sensitivity to the night, to the world about him, was doubly acute.

He realized—and it worried him—that perhaps he had come to depend too much on Sssuri's superior faculty of communication. It was time that he tried to use his own weaker powers to the utmost extent. So, while he climbed, Dalgard sent questing thoughts into the gloom. He located a nest of duck-dogs, those shy waterline fishers living in cliff holes. They were harmless and just settling down for the night. But of higher types of animals from which something might be learned—hoppers, runners—there were no traces. For all he was able to pick up, they might be climbing into blank nothingness.

And that in itself was ominous. Normally he should have been able to mind touch more than duck-dogs. The merpeople lived in peace with most of the higher fauna of their world, and a colony of hoppers, even a covey of moth birds, would settle in close by a mer tribe to garner in the remnants of feasts and for protection from the flying dragons and the other dangers they must face.

"*They* hunt all life," the first break in Sssuri's self-absorption came. "Where *they* walk the little, harmless peoples face only death. And so it has been here." He had pulled himself over the rim of the cliff, and through the dark Dalgard could hear him panting with the same effort which made his own lungs labor.

Just as the stench of the snake-devil's lair had betrayed its site, here disaster and death had an odor of its own. Dalgard retched before he could control throat and stomach muscles. But Sssuri was unmoved, as if he had expected this.

Then, to Dalgard's surprise the merman set up the first real call he had ever heard issue from that furred throat, a plaintive whistle which had a crooning, summoning note in it, akin to the mind touch in an odd fashion, yet audible. They sat in silence for a long moment, the human's ears as keen for any sound out of the night as those of his companion. Why did Sssuri not use the customary noiseless greeting of his race? When he beamed that inquiry, he met once again that strange, solid wall of non-acceptance which had enclosed the merman as they climbed. As if now there was danger to be feared from following the normal ways.

Again Sssuri whistled, and in that cry Dalgard heard a close resemblance to the flute tone of the night moth birds. Up the scale the notes ran with mournful persistence. When the answer came, the scout at first thought that the imitation had lured a moth bird, for the reply seemed to ripple right above their heads.

Sssuri stood up, and his hand dropped on Dalgard's shoulder, applying pressure which was both a warning and a summons, bringing the scout to his feet with as little noise as possible.

The horrible smell caught at his throat, and he was glad when the merman did not head inland toward the source of that odor, but started off along the edge of the cliff, one hand in Dalgard's to draw him along.

Twice more Sssuri paused to whistle, and each time he was answered by a signing note or two which seemed to reassure him.

Against the lighter expanse which was the sea, Dalgard saw the loom of a peak which projected above file general level of the island. Though he knew that the merpeople did not build aboveground, being adept in turning natural caves and crevices into the kind of living quarters they found most satisfactory, the barrenness of this particular rock top was forbidding.

Led by Sssuri, he threaded a tangled patch among outcrops, once-squeezing through a gap which scraped the flesh on his arms as he wriggled. Then the sky was blotted out, the last winking star disappeared, and he realized that he must have entered a cave of sorts, or was at least under an overhang.

The merman did not pause but padded on, tugging Dalgard along, the scout's boots scraping on the rough footing. The colonist was conscious now that they were on an incline, heading down into the heart of the island. They came to a stretch where Sssuri set his hands on holds, patiently shoved his feet into hollowed places, finding for him the ladder steps he could not see, which took him through a sweating, fearful journey of yards to another level, another sloping, downward way.

Here at long last was a fraction of light, not the violet glimmer which had illuminated the underground ways of those Others, but a ghostly radiance which he recognized as the lamps of the mermen—living creatures from the sea depths imprisoned in laboriously fashioned globes of crystal and kept in the caves for the light they yielded.

But still no mind touch! Never had Dalgard penetrated into the cave cities of the sea folk before without inquiries and open welcome lapping about him. Were they entering a place of massacre where no living merman remained? Yet there was that whistling which had led Sssuri to this place....

And at that moment a shrill keening note arose from the depths to ring in Dalgard's ears, startling him so that he almost lost his footing. Once again Sssuri made answer vocally—but no mind touch.

Then they rounded a curve, and the scout was able to see into the heart of the amphibian territory. This was a natural cave, as were all the merman's dwellings, but its walls had been smoothed and hung with the garlands of shells which they wove in their leisure into strange pictures. Silver-gray sand, smooth and dust-fine, covered the floor to the depth of a foot or more. And opening off the main chamber were small nooks, each marking the private storage place and holding of some family clan. It was a large place, and with a quick estimate Dalgard thought that it had been fashioned to harbor close to a hundred inhabitants, at least the nooks suggested that many. But gathered at the foot of the ledge they were descending, spears poised, were perhaps ten males, some hardly past cubhood, others showing the snowy shine of fur which was the badge of age. And behind them, drawn knives in their ready hands, were half again as many merwomen, forming a protecting wall before a crouching group of cubs.

Sssuri spoke to Dalgard. "Spread out your hands—empty—so that they may see them clearly!"

The scout obeyed. In the limited light his ten fingers were fans, and it was then that he understood the reason for such a move. If these mermen had not seen a colonist before, he might resemble Those Others in their eyes. But only his species on all Astra had five fingers, five toes, and that physical evidence might insure his safety now.

"Why do you bring a destroyer among us? Or do you offer him for our punishment, so that we can lay upon him the doom that his kind have earned?"

The question came with arrow force, and Dalgard held out his hands, hoping they would see the difference before one of those spears from below tore through his flesh.

"Look upon the hands of this—my knife brother—look upon his face. He is not of the race of those you hate, but rather one from the south. Have you of the northern reaches not heard of Those-Who-Help, Those-Who-Came-From-the-Stars?"

"We have heard." But there was no relaxing of tension, not a spear point wavered.

"Look upon his hands," Sssuri insisted. "Come into his mind, for he speaks with us so. And do *they* do that?"

Dalgard tried to throw open his mind, awaiting the trial. It came quickly, traces of inimical, alien thought, which changed as they touched his mind, reading there only all the friendliness he and his held for the sea people.

"He is not of *them*." The admission was grudging. As if they did not want to believe that. "Why comes one from the south to this place—now?"

There was an inflection to that "now" which was disturbing.

"After the manner of his people he seeks new things so that he may return and report to his Elders. Then he will receive the spear of manhood and be ready for the choosing of mates," Sssuri translated the reason for Dalgard's quest into the terms of his own people. "He has been my knife brother since we were cubs together, and so I journey with him. But here in the north we have found evil—"

His flow of thought was submerged by a band of hate so red that its impact upon the mind was almost a blow. Dalgard shook his head. He had known that the merpeople, aroused, were deadly fighters, fearless and crafty, and with a staying power beyond that of any human. But their rage was something he had not met before.

"*They* come once again—*they* burn with the fire—*They* are among our islands—"

A cub whimpered and a merwoman stooped to pat it to silence.

"Here they have killed with the fire—"

They did not elaborate upon that statement, and Dalgard had no wish for them to do so. He was still very glad that it had been dark when he had climbed to the top of that cliff, that he had not been able to see what his imagination told him lay there.

"Do *they* stay?" That was Sssuri.

"Not so. In their sky traveler they go to the land where lies the dark city. There they make much evil against the day when this shall be their land once more."

"But these lie if they think that." Another strong thought broke across the current of communication. "*We* are not now penned for their pleasure. We may flee into the sea once more, and there live as did our fathers' fathers, and they dare not follow us there—"

"Who knows?" It was Sssuri who raised that objection. "With their ancient knowledge once more theirs, even the depths of the sea may not be ours much longer. Do they not know how to ride upon the air?"

The knot of mer-warriors stirred. Several spears thudded butt down into the sand. And Sssuri accepted that as an invitation to descend, summoning Dalgard after him with a beckoning finger.

Later they sat in a circle in the cushioning gray powder, the two from the south eating dried fish and sea kelp, while Sssuri related, between mouthfuls, their recent adventures.

"Three times have *they* flown across these islands on their way to that city," the Elder of the pitifully decimated merman tribe told the explorers.

"But this time," broke in one of his companions, "they had with them a new ship—"

"A new ship?" Sssuri pounced upon that scrap of information.

"Yes. The ships of the air in which *they* travel are fashioned so"—with his knife point he drew a circle in the sand—"but this one was smaller and more in the likeness of a spear with a heavy point—thus"—he made a second sketch beside the first, and Dalgard and Sssuri leaned over to study it.

"That is unlike any of their ships that I have heard of," Sssuri agreed. "Even in the old tales of the Days Before the Burning there is nothing spoken of like that."

"It is true. Therefore we wait now for the coming of our scouts, who were set in hiding upon *their* sea rock of resting, that they may tell us more concerning this new ship. They should be here within this time of sleeping. Now, go you to rest, which you plainly have need of, and we shall call you when they come."

Dalgard was willing enough to stretch out in the sand in the shadows of the far end of the cave. Beyond him three cubs slumbered together, their arms about each other, and a feeling of peace was there such as he had not known since he left the stronghold of Homeport.

The weird glow of the imprisoned sea monsters gave light to the main part of the cave, and it might still have been night when the scout was shaken awake once more. A group of the merpeople were sitting together, and their thoughts interrupted each other as their excitement arose. Their spies must have returned.

Dalgard crossed to join that group, but it seemed to him that his welcome was not unqualified, and that some of the openness of the early hours of the night was lacking. He might have been once more under suspicion.

"Knife brother"—to Dalgard's sensitive mind that form of address from Sssuri was used for a special purpose: to underline the close bond between them—"listen to the words of Sssim who is a Hider-to-Watch on the island where *they* rest their ships during the voyage from one land to another." He drew Dalgard down beside him to face a young merman who was staring round-eyed at the colony scout.

"He is like—yet unlike"—his first wisp of thought meant nothing to the scout. "The strangers wear many coverings on their bodies as do *they*, and they had also coverings upon their heads. They were bigger. Also from their minds I learned that they are not of this world—"

"Not of this world!" Dalgard burst out in his own speech.

"There!" The spy was triumphant. "So did they talk to one another, not with the mind but by making mouth noises, different mouth noises from those that *they* make. Yes, they are like—but unlike this one."

"And these strangers flew the ship we have not seen before?"

"It is so. But they did not know the way and were guided by the globe. And at least one among them was distrustful of *those* and wished to be free to return to his own place. He walked by the rocks near my hiding place, and I read his thoughts. No, they were with *them*, but they are not *them*!"

"And now they have gone on to the city?" Sssuri probed.

"It was the way their ship flew."

"Like me," Dalgard repeated, and then the truth which might lie behind that exploded within his brain. "Terrans!" he breathed the word. Men of Pax perhaps who had come to hunt down the outlaws who had successfully eluded their rule on earth? But how had the colonists been traced? And why? Or were they other fugitives like themselves? So much, so very much of what the colonists should know of their past had been erased during the time of the Great Sickness twenty years after their landing. Then three fourths of the original immigrants had died. Only the children of the second generation and a handful of weakened Elders had remained. Knowledge was lost and some distorted by failing memories, old skills were gone. But if the new Terrans were in that city.... He had to know—to know and be able to warn his people. For the darkness of Pax was a memory they had *not* lost!

"I must see them," he said.

"That is true. And only you can tell us what manner of folk these strangers be," the merman chief agreed. "Therefore you shall go ashore with my warriors and look upon them—to tell us the truth. Also we must learn what *they* do here."

It was decided that using waterways known to the merpeople, one which Dalgard could also take wearing the diving equipment, a scouting party would head shoreward the next day, with the river itself providing the entrance into the heart of the forbidden territory.

12

ALIEN PATROL

Raf leaned back against the wall. Long since the actions of the aliens in the storage house had ceased to interest him, since they would not allow any of the Terrans to approach their plunder and he could not ask questions. Lablet continued to follow the officer about, vainly trying to understand his speech. And Hobart had taken his place by the upper entrance, his hand held stiffly across his body. The pilot knew that the captain was engaged in photographing all this activity with a wristband camera, hoping to make something of it later.

But Raf's own inclination was to slip out and do some exploring in those underground corridors beyond. Having remained where he was for a wearisome time, he noticed that his presence was now taken for granted by the hurrying aliens who brushed about him intent upon their assignments. And slowly he began to edge along the wall toward the other doorway. Once he froze as the officer strode by, Lablet in attendance. But what the painted warrior was looking for was a crystal box on a shelf to Raf's left. When he had pointed that out to an underling he was off again, and Raf was free to continue his crab's progress.

Luck favored him, for, as he reached the moment when he must duck out the portal, there was a sudden flurry at the other end of the chamber where four of the aliens, under a volley of orders, strove to move an unwieldy piece of intricate machinery.

Raf dodged around the door and flattened back against the wall of the room beyond. The moving bars of sun said that it was midday. But the room was empty save for the despoiled carcass, and there was no sign of the aliens who had been sent out to scout.

The Terran ran lightly down the narrow room to the second door, which gave on the lower pits beneath and the way to the arena. As he took that dark way, he drew his stun gun. Its bolt was intended to render the victim unconscious, not to kill. But what effect it might have on the giant reptiles was a question he hoped he would not be forced to answer, and he paused now and then to listen.

There were sounds, deceptive sounds. Noises as regular as footfalls, like a distant padded running. The aliens returning? Or the things they had gone to hunt? Raf crept on—out into the sunshine which filled the arena.

For the first time he studied the enclosure and recognized it for what it was—a place in which savage and bloody entertainments could be provided for the population of the city—and it merely confirmed his opinion of the aliens and all their ways.

The temptation to explore the city was strong. He eyed the grilles speculatively. They could be climbed—he was sure of that. Or he could try some other of the various openings about the sanded area. But as he hesitated over his choice, he heard something from behind. This was no unidentifiable noise, but a scream which held both terror and pain. It jerked him around, sent him running back almost before he thought.

But the scream did not come again. However there were other sounds—snuffing whines—a scrabbling—

Raf found himself in the round room walled by the old prison cells. Stabs of light shot through the gloom, thrusting into a roiling black mass which had erupted through one of the entrances and now held at bay one of the alien warriors. Three or four of the black creatures ringed the alien in, moving with speed that eluded the bolts of light he shot from his weapon, keeping him cornered and from escape, while their fellows worried another alien limp and defenseless on the floor.

It was impossible to align the sights of his stun gun with any of those flitting shadows, Raf discovered. They moved as quickly as a ripple across a pond. He snapped the button on the hand grip to "spray" and proceeded to use the full strength of the charge across the group on the floor.

For several seconds he was afraid that the stun ray would prove to have no effect on the alien metabolism of the creatures, for their weaving, tearing activity did not cease. Then one after another dropped away from the center mass and lay unmoving on the floor. Seeing that he could control them, Raf turned his attention to the others about the standing warrior.

Again he sent the spray wide, and they subsided. As the last curled on the pavement, the alien moved forward and, with a snarl, deliberately turned the full force of his beam weapon on each of the attackers. But Raf plowed on through the limp pile to the warrior they had pulled down.

There was no hope of helping him—death had come with a wide tear in his throat. Raf averted his eyes from the body. The other warrior was methodically killing the stunned animals. And his action held such vicious cruelty that Raf did not want to watch.

When he looked again at the scene, it was to find the narrow barrel of the strange weapon pointed at him. Paying no attention to his dead comrade, the alien was advancing on the Terran as if in Raf he saw only another enemy to be burned down.

Moves drilled in him by long hours of weary practice came almost automatically to the pilot. The stun gun faced the alien rifle sight to sight. And it seemed that the warrior had developed a hearty respect for the Terran arm during the past few minutes, for he slipped his weapon back to the crook of his arm, as if he did not wish Raf to guess he had used it to threaten.

The pilot had no idea what to do now. He did not wish to return to the storehouse. And he believed that the alien was not going to let him go off alone. The ferocity of the creatures now heaped about them had been sobering, an effective warning against venturing alone in these underground ways.

His dilemma was solved by the entrance of a party of aliens from another doorway. They stopped short at the sight of the battlefield, and their leader descended upon the surviving scout for an explanation, which was made with gestures Raf was able to translate in part.

The alien had been far down one of the neighboring corridors with his dead companion when they had been tracked by the pack and had managed to reach this point before they were attacked. For some reason Raf could not understand, the aliens had preferred to flee rather than to face the menace of the hunters. But they had not been fast enough and had been trapped here. The gesturing hands then indicated Raf, acted out the battle which had ensued.

Crossing to the Terran pilot, the alien officer held out his hand and motioned for Raf to surrender his weapon. The pilot shook his head. Did they think him so simple that he would disarm himself at the mere asking? Especially since the warrior had rounded on him like that only a few moments before? Nor did he holster his gun. If they wanted to take it by force just let them try such a move!

His determination to resist must have gotten across to the leader, for he did not urge obedience to his orders. Instead he waved the Terran to join his own party. And since Raf had no reason not to, he did. Leaving the dead, both alien and enemy, where they had fallen, the warriors took another way out of the underground maze, a way which brought them out into a street running to the river.

Here the party spread out, paying close attention to the pavement, as if they were engaged in tracking something. Raf saw impressed in one patch of earth a print dried by the sun, left by one of the reptiles. And there were smaller tracks he could not identify. All were inspected carefully, but none of them appeared to be what his companions sought.

They trotted up and down along the river bank, and from what he had already observed concerning the aliens, Raf thought that the leader, at least, was showing exasperation and irritation. They expected to find something—it was not there—but it had to be! And they were fast reaching the point where they wanted to produce it themselves to justify the time spent in hunting for it.

Ruthlessly they rayed to death any creature their dragnet drove into the open, leaving feebly kicking bodies of the furry, long-legged beasts Raf had first seen after the landing of the spacer. He could not understand the reason for such wholesale extermination, since certainly the rabbitlike rodents were harmless.

In the end they gave up their quest and circled back to come out near the field where the flitter and the globe rested. When the Terran flyer came into sight, Raf left the party and hurried toward it. Soriki waved a welcoming hand.

"'Bout time one of you showed up. What are they doing— toting half the city here to load into that thing?"

Raf looked along the other's pointing finger. A party of aliens towing a loaded dolly were headed for the gaping hatch of the globe, while a second party and an empty conveyance passed them on the way back to the storehouse.

"They are emptying a warehouse, or trying to."

"Well, they act as if Old Time himself was heating their tails with a rocket flare. What's the big hurry?"

"Somebody's been here." Swiftly Raf outlined what he had seen in the city, and ended by describing the hunt in which he had taken an unwilling part. "I'm hungry," he ended and went to burrow for a ration pack.

"So," mused Soriki as Raf chewed the stuff which never had the flavor of fresh provisions, "somebody's been trying to beat the painted lads to it. The furry people?"

"It was a spear shaft they found broken with the dead lizard thing," Raf commented. "And some of those on the island were armed with spears—"

"Must be good fighters if, armed with spears, they brought down a reptile as big as you say. It was big, wasn't it?"

Raf stared at the city, a square of half-eaten concentrate in his fingers. Yes, that was a puzzler. The dead monster would be more than *he* would care to tackle without a blaster. And yet it was dead, with a smashed spear for evidence as to the manner of killing.

All those others dead in the arena, too. How large a party had invaded the city? Where were they now?

"I'd like to know," he was speaking more to himself than to the com-tech, "how they *did* do it. No other bodies—"

"Those could have been taken away by their friends," Soriki suggested. "But if they're still hanging about, I hope they won't believe that we're bigger and better editions of the painted lads. I don't want a spear through me!"

Raf, remembering the maze of lanes and streets—bordered by buildings which could provide hundreds of lurking places for attackers—which he had threaded with the confidence of ignorance earlier that day, began to realize why the aliens had been so nervous. Had a sniper with a blast rifle been stationed at a vantage point somewhere on the roofs today none of them would ever have returned to this field. And even a few spacemen with good cover and accurate throwing aim could have cut down their number a quarter or a third. He was developing a strong distaste for those structures. And he had no intention of returning to the city again.

He lounged about with Soriki for the rest of the afternoon, watching the ceaseless activity of the aliens. It was plain that they were intent upon packing into the cargo hold of their ship everything they could wrest from the storage house. As if they must make this trip count double. Was that because they had discovered that their treasure house was no longer inviolate?

In the late afternoon Hobart and Lablet came back with one of the work teams. Lablet was still excited, full of what he had seen, deduced, or guessed during the day. But the captain was very quiet and sober, and he unstrapped the wrist camera as soon as he reached the flitter, turning it over to Soriki.

"Run that through the ditto," he ordered. "I want two records as soon as we can get them!"

The com-tech's eyebrows slid up, "Think you might lose one, sir?"

"I don't know. Anyway, we'll play it safe with double records." He accepted the ration pack Raf had brought out for him. But he did not unwrap it at once; instead he stared at the globe, digging the toe of his space boot into the soil as if he were grinding something to powder.

"They're operating under full jets," he commented. "As if they were about due to be jumped—"

"They told us that this was territory now held by their enemies," Lablet reminded him.

"And who are these mysterious enemies?" the captain wanted to know. "Those animals back on that island?"

Raf wanted to say yes, but Lablet broke in with a question concerning what had happened to him, and the pilot outlined his adventures of the day, not forgetting to give emphasis to the incident in the celled room when the newly rescued alien had turned upon him.

"Naturally they are suspicious," Lablet countered, "but for a people who lack space flight, I find them unusually open-minded and ready to accept us, strange as we must seem to them."

"Ditto done, Captain." Soriki stepped out of the flitter, the wrist camera dangling from his fingers.

"Good." But Hobart did not buckle the strap about his arm once more, neither did he pay any attention to Lablet. Instead, apparently coming to some decision, he swung around to face Raf.

"You went out with that scouting party today. Think you could join them again, if you see them moving for another foray?"

"I could try."

"Sure," Soriki chuckled, "they couldn't do any more than pop him back at us. What do you think about them, sir? Are they fixing to blast us?"

But the captain refused to be drawn. "I'd just like to have a record of any more trips they make." He handed the camera to Raf. "Put that on and don't forget to trigger it if you do go. I don't believe they'll go out tonight. They aren't too fond of being out in the open in darkness. We saw that last night. But keep an eye on them in the morning—"

"Yes, sir." Raf buckled on the wristband. He wished that Hobart would explain just what he was to look for, but the captain appeared to think that he had made everything perfectly plain. And he walked off with Lablet, heading to the globe, as if there was nothing more to be said.

Soriki stretched. "I'd say we'd better take it watch and watch," he said slowly. "The captain may think that they won't go off in the dark, but we don't know everything about them. Suppose we just keep an eye on them, and then you'll be ready to tail—"

Raf laughed. "Tailing would be it. I don't think I'll have a second invitation and if I get lost—"

But Soriki shook his head. "That you won't. At least if you do—I'm going to make a homer out of you. Just tune in your helmet buzzer."

It needed a com-tech to think of a thing like that! A small adjustment to the earphones built into his helmet, and Soriki, operating the flitter com, could give him a guide as efficient as the spacer's radar! He need not fear being lost in the streets should he lose touch with those he was spying upon.

"You're on course!" He pulled off his helmet and then glanced up to find Soriki smiling at him.

"Oh, we're not such a bad collection of space bums. Maybe you'll find that out someday, boy. They breezed you into this flight right out of training, didn't they?"

"Just about," Raf admitted cautiously, on guard as ever against revealing too much of himself. After all, his experience was part of his record, which was open to anyone on board the spacer. Yes, he was not a veteran; they must all know that.

"Someday you'll lose a little of that suspicion," the com-tech continued, "and find out it isn't such a bad old world after all. Here, let's see if you're on the beam." He took the helmet out of Raf's hands and, drawing a small case of delicate instruments from his belt pouch, unscrewed the ear plates of the com device and made some adjustments. "Now that will keep you on the buzzer without bursting your eardrums. Try it."

Raf fastened on the helmet and started away from the flitter. The buzzer which he had expected to roar in his ears was only a faint drone, and above it he could easily hear other sounds. Yet it was there, and he tested it by a series of loops away from the flyer. Each time as he came on the true beam he was rewarded by a deepening of the muted note. Yes, he could be a homer with that, and at the same time be alert to any other noise in his vicinity.

"That's it!" He paid credit where it was due. But he was unable to break his long habit of silence. Something within him still kept him wary of the com-tech's open friendliness.

None of the aliens approached the flitter as the shadows began to draw in. The procession of moving teams stopped, and most of the burden-bearing warriors withdrew to the globe and stayed there. Soriki pointed this out.

"They're none too sure, themselves. Look as if they are closing up for the night."

Indeed it did. The painted men had hauled up their ramp, the hatch in the globe closed with a definite snap. Seeing that, the com-tech laughed.

"We have a double reason for a strict watch. Suppose whatever they've been looking for jumps *us*? They're not worrying over that it now appears."

So they took watch and watch, three hours on and three hours in rest. When it came Raf's turn he did not remain sitting in the flitter, listening to the com-tech's heavy breathing, but walked a circular beat which took him into the darkness of the night in a path about the flyer. Overhead the stars were sharp and clear, glittering gem points. But in the dead city no light showed, and he was sure that no aliens camped there tonight.

He was sleeping when Soriki's grasp on his shoulder brought him to that instant alertness he had learned on field maneuvers half the Galaxy away.

"Business," the com-tech's voice was not above a whisper as he leaned over the pilot. "I think they are on the move."

The light was the pale gray of pre-dawn. Raf pulled himself up with caution to look at the globe. The com-tech was right. A dark opening showed on the alien ship; they had released their hatch. He fastened his tunic, buckled on his equipment belt and helmet, strapped his boots.

"Here they come!" Soriki reported. "One—two—five—no, six of them. And they're heading for the city. No dollies with them, but they're all armed."

Together the Terrans watched that patrol of alien warriors, their attitude suggesting that they hoped to pass unseen, hurry toward the city. Then Raf slipped out of the flyer. His dark clothing in this light should render him largely invisible.

Soriki waved encouragingly and the pilot answered with a quick salute before he sped after his quarry.

13

A HOUND IS LOOSED

Dalgard's feet touched gravel; he waded cautiously to the bank, where a bridge across the river made a concealing shadow on the water. None of the mermen had accompanied him this far. Sssuri, as soon as his human comrade had started for the storage city, had turned south to warn and rally the tribes. And the merpeople of the islands had instituted a loose chain of communication, which led from a clump of water reeds some two miles back to the seashore, and so out to the islands. Better than any of the now legendary coms of his Terran forefathers were these minds of the spies in hiding, who could pick up the racing thoughts beamed to them and pass them on to their fellows.

Although there were no signs of life about the city, Dalgard moved with the same care that he would have used in penetrating a snake-devil's lair. In the first hour of dawn he had contacted a hopper. The small beast had been frightened almost out of coherent thought, and Dalgard had had to spend some time in allaying that terror to get a fractional idea of what might be going on in this countryside.

Death—the hopper's terror had come close to insanity. Killers had come out of the sky, and they were burning—

burning—All living things were fleeing before them. And in that moment Dalgard had been forced to give up his plan for an unseen spy ring, which would depend upon the assistance of the animals. His information must come via his own eyes and ears.

So he kept on, posting the last of the mermen in his mental relay well away from the city, but swimming upstream himself. Now that he was here, he could see no traces of the invaders. Since they could not have landed their sky ships in the thickly built-up section about the river, it must follow that their camp lay on the outskirts of the metropolis.

He pulled himself out of the water. Bow and arrows had been left behind with the last merman; he had only his sword-knife for protection. But he was not there to fight, only to watch and wait. Pressing the excess moisture out of his scant clothing, he crept along the shore. If the strangers were using the streets, it might be well to get above them. Speculatively he eyed the buildings about him as he entered the city.

Dalgard continued to keep at street level for two blocks, darting from doorway to shadowed doorway, alert not only to any sound but to any flicker of thought. He was reasonably sure, however, that the aliens would be watching and seeking only for the merpeople. Though they were not telepathic as their former slaves, Those Others were able to sense the near presence of a merman, so that the sea people dared not communicate while within danger range of the aliens without betraying themselves. It was the fact that he was of a different species, therefore possibly immune to such detection, which had brought Dalgard into the city.

He studied the buildings ahead. Among them was a cone-shaped structure which might have been the base of a tower that had had all stories above the third summarily amputated. It was ornamented with a series of bands in high relief, bands bearing the color script of the aliens. This was the nearest answer to his problem. However the scout did not move toward it until after a long moment of both visual and mental inspection of his surroundings. But that inspection did not reach some twelve streets away where another crouched to watch. Dalgard ran lightly to the tower at the same moment that Raf shifted his weight from one foot to the other behind a parapet as he spied upon the knot of aliens gathered below him in the street....

The pilot had followed them since that early morning hour when Soriki had awakened him. Not that the chase had led him far in distance. Most of the time he had spent in waiting just as he was doing now. At first he had believed that they were searching for something, for they had ventured into several buildings, each time to emerge conferring, only to hunt out another and invade it. Since they always returned with empty hands, he could not believe that they were out for further loot. Also they moved with more confidence than they had shown the day before. That confidence led Raf to climb above them so that he could watch them with less chance of being seen in return.

It had been almost noon when they had at last come into this section. If two of them had not remained idling on the street as the long moments crept by, he would have believed that they had given him the slip, that he was now a cat watching a deserted mouse hole. But at the moment they were coming back, carrying something.

Raf leaned as far over the parapet as he dared, trying to catch a better look at the flat, boxlike object two of them had deposited on the pavement. Whatever it was either needed some adjustment or they were attempting to open it with poor success, for they had been busied about it for what seemed an unusually long time. The pilot licked dry lips and wondered what would happen if he swung down there and just walked in for a look-see. That idea was hardening into resolution when suddenly the group below drew quickly apart, leaving the box sitting alone as they formed a circle about it.

There was a puff of white vapor, a protesting squawk, and the thing began to rise in jerks as if some giant in the sky was pulling at it spasmodically. Raf jumped back. Before he could return to his vantage point, he saw it rise above the edge of the parapet, reach a level five or six feet above his head, hovering there. It no longer climbed; instead it began to swing back and forth, describing in each swing a wider stretch of space.

Back and forth—watching it closely made him almost dizzy. What was its purpose? Was it a detection device, to locate him? Raf's hand went to his stun gun. What effect its rays might have on the box he had no way of knowing, but at that moment he was sorely tempted to try the beam out, with the oscillating machine as his target.

The motion of the floating black thing became less violent, its swoop smoother as if some long-idle motor was now working more as its builders had intended it to perform. The swing made wide circles, graceful glides as the thing explored the air currents.

Searching—it was plainly searching for something. Just as plainly it could not be hunting for him, for his presence on that roof would have been uncovered at once. But the machine was—it must be—out of sight of the warriors in the street. How could they keep in touch with it if it located what they sought? Unless it had some built-in signaling device.

Determined to keep it in sight, Raf risked a jump from the parapet of the building where he had taken cover to another roof beyond, running lightly across that as the hound bobbed and twisted, away from its masters, out across the city in pursuit of some mysterious quarry....

$$* \quad * \quad * \quad * \quad *$$

The climb which had looked so easy from the street proved to be more difficult when Dalgard actually made it. His hours of swimming in the river, the night of broken rest, had drained his strength more than he had known. He was panting as he flattened himself against the wall, his feet on one of the protruding bands of colored carving, content to rest before reaching for another hold. To all appearances the city about him was empty of life and, except for the certainty of the merpeople that the alien ship and its strange companion had landed here, he would have believed that he was on a fruitless quest.

Grimly, his lower lip caught between his teeth, the scout began to climb once more, the sun hot on his body, drawing sweat to dampen his forehead and his hands. He did not pause again but kept on until he stood on the top of the shortened tower. The roof here was not flat but sloped inward to a cuplike depression, where he could see the outline of a round opening, perhaps a door of sorts. But at that moment he was too winded to do more than rest.

There was a drowsiness in that air. He was tempted to curl up where he sat and turn his rest into the sleep his body craved. It was in that second or so of time when he was beginning to relax, to forget the tenseness which had gripped him since his return to this ill-omened place, that he touched—

Dalgard stiffened as if one of his own poisoned arrows had pricked his skin. Rapport with the merpeople, with the hoppers and the runners, was easy, familiar. But this was no such touch. It was like contacting something which was icy cold, inimical from birth, something which he could never meet on a plain of understanding. He snapped off mind questing at that instant and huddled where he was, staring up into the blank turquoise of the sky, waiting—for what he did not know. Unless it was for that other mind to follow and ferret out his hiding place, to turn him inside out and wring from him everything he ever knew or hoped to learn.

As time passed in long breaths, and he was not so invaded, he began to think that while he had been aware of contact, the other had not. And, emboldened, he sent out a tracer. Unconsciously, as the tracer groped, he pivoted his body. It lay—there!

At the second touch he withdrew in the same second, afraid of revelation. But as he returned to probe delicately, ready to flee at the first hint that the other suspected, his belief in temporary safety grew. To his disappointment he could not pierce beyond the outer wall of identity. There was a living creature of a high rate of intelligence, a creature alien to his own thought processes, not too far away. And though his attempts to enter into closer communication grew bolder, he could not crack the barrier which kept them apart. He had long known that contact with the merpeople was on a lower, a far lower, band than they used when among themselves, and that they were only able to "talk" with the colonists because for generations they had exchanged thought symbols with the hoppers and other unlike species. They had been frank in admitting that while Those Others could be aware of their presence through telepathic means, they could not exchange thoughts. So now, his own band, basically strange to this planet, might well go unnoticed by the once dominant race of Astra.

They—or him—or it—were over in that direction, Dalgard was sure of that. He faced northwest and saw for the first time, about a mile away, the swelling of the globe. If the strange flyer reported by the merpeople was beside it, he could not distinguish it from this distance. Yet he was sure the mind he had located was closer to him than that ship.

Then he saw it—a black object rising by stiff jerks into the air as if it were being dragged upward against its inclination. It was too small to be a flyer of any sort. Long ago the colonists had patched together a physical description of Those Others which had assured them that the aliens were close to them in general characteristics and size. No, that couldn't be carrying a passenger. Then what—or why?

The object swung out in a gradually widening circle. Dalgard held to the walled edge of the roof. Something within him suggested that it would be wiser to seek some less open space, that there was danger in that flying box. He released his hold and went to the trap door. It took only a minute to fit his fingers into round holes and tug. Its stubborn resistance gave, and stale air whooshed out in his face as it opened.

In his battle with the door Dalgard had ignored the box, so he was startled when, with a piercing whistle, almost too high on the scale for his ears to catch, the thing suddenly swooped into a screaming dive, apparently heading straight for him. Dalgard flung himself through the trap door, luckily landing on one of the steep, curved ramps. He lost his balance and slid down into the dark, trying to brake his descent with his hands, the eerie screech of the box trumpeting in his ears.

There was little light in this section of the cone building, and he was brought up with bruising force against a blank wall two floors below where he had so unceremoniously entered. As he lay in the dark trying to gasp some breath back into his lungs, he could still hear the squeal. Was it summoning? There was no time to be lost in getting away.

On his hands and knees the scout crept along what must have been a short hall until he found a second descending ramp, this one less steep than the first, so that he was able to keep to his feet while using it. And the gloom of the next floor was broken by odd scraps of light which showed through pierced portions of the decorative bands. The door was there, a locking bar across it.

Dalgard did not try to shift that at once, although he laid his hands upon it. If the box was a hound for hunters, had it already drawn its masters to this building? Would he open the door only to be faced by the danger he wished most to avoid? Desperately he tried to probe with the mind touch. But he could not find the alien band. Was that because the hunters could control their minds as they crept up? His kind knew so little of Those Others, and the merpeople's hatred of their ancient masters was so great that they tended to avoid rather than study them.

The scout's sixth sense told him that nothing waited outside. But the longer he lingered with that beacon overhead the slimmer his chances would be. He must move and quickly. Sliding back the bar, he opened the door a crack and looked out into a deserted street. There was another doorway to take shelter in some ten feet or so farther along, beyond that an alley wall overhung by a balcony. He marked these refuges and went out to make his first dash to safety.

Nothing stirred, and he sprinted. There came again that piercing shriek to tear his ears as the floating box dived at him. He swerved away from the doorway to dart on under the balcony, sure now that he must keep moving, but under cover so that the black thing could not pounce. If he could find some entrance into the underground ways such as those that ran from the arena—But now he was not even sure in which direction the arena stood, and he dared no longer climb to look over the surrounding territory.

He touched the alien mind! They *were* moving in, following the lead of their hound. He must not allow himself to be cornered. The scout fought down a surge of panic, attempted to battle the tenseness which tied his nerves. He must not run mindlessly either. That was probably just what they wanted him to do. So he stood under the balcony and tried not to listen to the shrilling of the box as he studied the strip of alley.

This was a narrow side way, and he had not made the wisest of choices in entering it, for not much farther ahead it was bordered with smooth walls protecting what had once been gardens. He had no way of telling whether the box would actually attack him if he were caught in the open—to put that to the test was foolhardy—nor could he judge its speed of movement.

The walls.... A breeze which blew up the lane carried with it the smell of the river. There was a slim chance that it might end in water, and he had a feeling that if he could reach the stream he would be able to baffle the hunters. He did not have long to make up his mind—the aliens were closer.

Lightly Dalgard ran under the length of the balcony, turned sharply as he reached the end of its protecting cover, and leaped. His fingers gripped the ornamental grillwork, and he was able to pull himself up and over to the narrow runway. A canopy was still over his head, and there came a bump against it as the baffled box thumped. So it would try to knock him off if it could get the chance! That was worth knowing.

He looked over the walls. They guarded masses of tangled vegetation grown through years of neglect into thick mats. And those promised a way of escape, if he could reach them. He studied the windows, the door opening onto the balcony. With the hilt of his sword-knife he smashed his way into the house, to course swiftly through the rooms to the lower floor, and find the entrance to the garden.

Facing that briary jungle on the ground level was a little daunting. To get through it would be a matter of cutting his way. Could he do it and escape that bobbing, shrilling thing in the air? A trace of pebbled path gave him a ghost of a chance, and he knew that these shrubs tended to grow upward and not mass until they were several feet above the ground.

Trusting to luck, Dalgard burrowed into the green mass, slashing with his knife at anything which denied him entrance. He was swallowed up in a strange dim world wherein dead shrubs and living were twined together to form a roof, cutting off the light and heat of the sun. From the sour earth, sliming his hands and knees, arose an overpowering stench of decay and disturbed mold. In the dusk he had to wait for his eyes to adjust before he could mark the line of the old path he had taken for his guide.

Fortunately, after the first few feet, he discovered that the tunneled path was less obstructed than he had feared. The thick mat overhead had kept the sun from the ground and killed off all the lesser plants so that it was possible to creep along a fairly open strip. He was conscious of the chitter of insects, but no animals lingered here. Under him the ground grew more moist and the mold was close to mud in consistency. He dared to hope that this meant he was either approaching the river or some garden stream feeding into the larger flood.

Somewhere the squeal of the hunter kept up a steady cry, but, unless the foliage above him was distorting that sound, Dalgard believed that the box was no longer directly above him. Had he in some way thrown it off his trail?

He found his stream, a thread of water, hardly more than a series of scummy pools with the vegetation still meeting almost solidly over it. And it brought him to a wall with a drain through which he was sure he could crawl. Disliking to venture into that cramped darkness, but seeing no other way out, the scout squirmed forward in slime and muck, feeling the rasp of rough stone on his shoulders as he made his worm's progress into the unknown.

Once he was forced to halt and, in the dark, loosen and pick out stones embedded in the mud bottom narrowing the passage. On the other side of that danger point, he was free to wriggle on. Could the box trace him now? He had no idea of the principle on which it operated; he could only hope.

Then before him he saw the ghostly gray of light and squirmed with renewed vigor—to be faced then by a grille, beyond which was the open world. Once more his knife came into use as he pried and dug at the barrier. He worked for long moments until the grille splashed out into the sluggish current a foot or so below, and then he made ready to lower himself into the same flood.

It was only because he was a trained hunter that he avoided death in that moment. Some instinct made him dodge even as he slipped through, and the hurtling black box did not strike true at the base of his brain but raked along his scalp, tearing the flesh and sending him tumbling unconscious into the brown water.

14

THE PRISONER

Raf was two streets away from the circling box but still able to keep it in sight when its easy glide stopped, and, in a straight line, it swooped toward a roof emitting a shrill, rising whistle. It rose again a few seconds later as if baffled, but it continued to hover at that point, keening forth its warning. The pilot reached the next building, but a street still kept him away from the conical structure above which the box now hung.

Undecided, he stayed where he was. Should he go down to street level and investigate? Before he had quite made up his mind he saw the foremost of the alien scouting party round into the thoroughfare below and move purposefully at the cone tower, weapons to the fore. Judging by their attitude, the box had run to earth there the prey they had been searching for.

But it wasn't to be so easy. With another eerie howl the machine soared once more and bobbed completely over the cone to the street which must lie beyond it. Raf knew that he could not miss the end of the chase and started on a detour along the roof tops which should bring him to a vantage point. By the time he had made that journey he found himself on a warehouse roof which projected over the edge of the river.

From a point farther downstream a small boat was putting out. Two of the aliens paddled while a third crouched in the bow. A second party was picking its way along the bank some distance away, both groups seemingly heading toward a point a building or two to the left of the one where Raf had taken cover.

He heard the shrilling of the box, saw it bobbing along a line toward the river. But in that direction there was only a mass of green. The end to the weird chase came so suddenly that he was not prepared, and it was over before he caught a good look at the quarry. Something moved down on the river bank and in that same instant the box hurtled earthward as might a spear. It struck, and the creature who had just crawled out— out of the ground as far as Raf could see—toppled into the stream. As the waters closed over the body, the box slued around and came to rest on the bank. The party in the boat sent their small craft flying toward the spot where the crawler had sunk.

One of the paddlers abandoned his post and slipped over the side, diving into the oily water. He made two tries before he was successful and came to the surface with the other in tow. They did not try to heave the unconscious captive into the boat, merely kept the lolling head above water as they turned downstream once more and vanished from Raf's sight around the end of a pier, while the second party on the bank reclaimed the now quiet box and went off.

But Raf had seen enough to freeze him where he was for a moment. The creature which had popped out of the ground only to be struck by the box and knocked into the river—he would take oath on the fact that it was not one of the furred animals he had seen on the sea island. Surely it had been smooth-skinned, not unlike the aliens in conformation—one of their own kind they had been hunting down, a criminal or a rebel?

Puzzled, the pilot moved along from roof to roof, trying to pick up the trail of the party in the boat, but as far as he could now see, the river was bare. If they had come ashore anywhere along here, they had simply melted into the city. At last he was forced to use the homing beam, and it guided him back across the deserted metropolis to the field.

There was still activity about the globe; they were bringing in the loot from the warehouse, but Lablet and Hobart stood by the flitter. As the pilot came up to them, the captain looked up eagerly.

"What happened?"

Raf sensed that there had been some change during his absence, that Hobart was looking to him for an explanation to make clear happenings here. He told his story of the hunt and its ending, the capture of the stranger. Lablet nodded as he finished.

"That is the reason for this, you may depend upon it, Captain. One of their own people is at the bottom of it."

"Of what?" Raf wanted to ask, but Soriki did it for him.

Hobart smiled grimly. "We are all traveling back together. Take off in the early morning. For some reason they wanted us out of the globe in a hurry—practically shoved us out half an hour ago."

Though the Terrans kept a watch on the larger ship as long

as the light lasted, the darkness defeated them. They did not see the prisoner being taken aboard. Yet none of them doubted that sometime during the dusky hours it had been done.

It was barely dawn when the globe took off the next day, and Raf brought the flitter up on its trail, heading westward into the sea wind. Below them the land held no signs of life. They swept over the deserted, terraced city that was the gateway to the guarded interior, flew back over the line of sea islands. Raf climbed higher, not caring to go too near the island where the aliens had wrought their terrible vengeance on the trip out. And all four of the Terrans knew relief, though they might not admit it to each other, when once more Soriki was able to establish contact with the distant spacer.

"Turn north, sir?" the pilot suggested. "I could ride her beam in from here—we don't have to follow them home." He wanted to do that so badly it was almost a compulsion to make his hand move on the controls. And when Hobart did not answer at once, he was sure that the captain would give that very order, taking them out of the company of those he had never trusted.

But Lablet spoiled that. "We have their word, Captain. That anti-grav unit that they showed us last night alone—"

So Hobart shook his head, and they meekly continued on the path set by the globe across the ocean.

As the hours passed Raf's inner uneasiness grew. For some queer reason which he could not define to himself or explain to anyone else, he was now possessed by an urgency to trail the globe which transcended and then erased his dislike of the aliens. It was as if some appeal for help was being broadcast from the other ship, drawing him on. It was then that he began to question his assumption that the prisoner was one of them.

Over and over again in his mind he tried to re-picture the capture as he had witnessed it from the building just too far away and at slightly the wrong angle for a clear view. He would swear that the body he had seen tumble into the flood had not been furred, that much he was sure of. But clothing, yes, there had been clothing. Not—his mind suddenly produced that one scrap of memory—not the bandage windings of the aliens. And hadn't the skin been fairer? Was there another race on this continent, one they had not been told about?

When they at last reached the shore of the western continent and finally the home city of the aliens, the globe headed back to its berth, not in the roof cradle from which it had arisen, but sinking into the building itself. Raf brought the flitter down on a roof as close to the main holding of the painted people as he could get. None of the aliens came near them. It seemed that they were to be ignored. Hobart paced along the flat roof, and Soriki sat in the flyer, nursing his com, intent upon the slender thread of beam which tied them to the parent ship so many miles away.

"I don't understand it." Lablet's voice arose almost plaintively. "They were so very persuasive about our accompanying them. They were eager to have us see their treasures—"

Hobart swung around. "Somehow the balance of power has changed," he observed, "in their favor. I'd give anything to know more about that prisoner of theirs. You're sure it wasn't one of the furry people?" he asked Raf, as if hoping against hope that the pilot would reply in doubt.

"Yes, sir." Raf hesitated. Should he air his suspicions, that the captive was not of the same race as his captors either? But what proof had he beyond a growing conviction that he could not substantiate?

"A rebel, a thief—" Lablet was ready to dismiss it as immaterial. "Naturally they would be upset if they were having trouble with one of their own men. But to leave now, just when we are on the verge of new discoveries—That anti-gravity unit alone is worth our whole trip! Imagine being able to return to earth with the principle of that!"

"Imagine being able to return to earth with our skins on our backs," was Soriki's whispered contribution. "If we had the sense of a Venusian water nit, we'd blast out of here so quick our tail fumes'd take off with us!"

Privately Raf concurred, but the urge to know more about the mysterious prisoner was still pricking at him, until he, contrary to his usual detachment, felt driven to discover all that he could. It was almost, but Raf shied away from that wild idea, it was almost as if he were hearing a voiceless cry for aid, as if his mind was one of Soriki's coms tuned in on an unknown wave length. He was angrily impatient with himself for that fantastic supposition. At the same time, another part of his mind, as he walked to the edge of the roof and looked out at the buildings he knew were occupied by the aliens, was busy examining the scene as if he intended to crawl about on roof tops on a second scouting expedition.

Finally the rest decided that Lablet and Hobart were to try to establish contact with the aliens once more. After they had gone, Raf opened a compartment in the flitter, the contents of which were his particular care. He squatted on his heels and surveyed the neatly stowed objects inside thoughtfully. A survival kit depended a great deal on the type of terrain in which the user was planning to survive—an aquatic world would require certain basic elements, a frozen tundra others—but there were a few items common to every emergency, and those were now at Raf's fingertips. The blast bombs, sealed into their pexilod cases, guaranteed to stop all the attackers that Terran explorers had so far met on and off worlds, a coil of rope hardly thicker than a strand of knitting yarn but of inconceivable toughness and flexibility, an aid kit with endurance drugs and pep pills which could keep a man on his feet and going long after food and water failed. He had put them all in their separate compartments.

For a long moment he hunkered there, studying the assortment. And then, almost as if some will other than his own was making a choice, he reached out. The rope curled about his waist under his tunic so tautly that its presence could not be detected without a search, blast bombs went into the sealed seam pocket on his breast, and two flat containers with their capsules were tucked away in his belt pouch. He snapped the door shut and got to his feet to discover Soriki watching him. Only for a moment was Raf disconcerted. He knew that he would not be able to explain why he must do what he was going to do. There was no reason why he should. Soriki, except for being a few years his senior, had no authority over him. He was not under the com-tech's orders.

"Another trip into the blue?"

The pilot replied to that with a nod.

"Somehow, boy, I don't think anything's going to stop you, so why waste my breath? But use your homer—and your eyes!"

Raf paused. There was an unmistakable note of friendliness in the com-tech's warning. Almost he was tempted to try and explain. But how could one make plain feelings for which there was no sensible reason? Sometimes it was better to be quiet.

"Don't dig up more than you can rebury." That warning, in the slang current when they had left Terra, was reassuring simply because it was of the earth he knew. Raf grinned. But he did not head toward the roof opening and the ramp inside the building. Instead he set a course he had learned in the other city, swinging down to the roof of the neighboring structure, intent on working away from the inhabited section of the town before he went into the streets.

Either the aliens had not set any watch on the Terrans or else all their interest was momentarily engaged elsewhere. Raf, having gone three or four blocks in the opposite direction to his goal, made his way through a silent, long-deserted building to the street without seeing any of the painted people. In his ear buzzed the comforting hum of the com, tying him with the flitter and so, in a manner, to safety.

He knew that the alien community had gathered in and around the central building they had visited. To his mind the prisoner was now either in the headquarters of the warriors, where the globe had been berthed, or had been taken to the administration building. Whether he could penetrate either stronghold was a question Raf did not yet face squarely.

But the odd something which tugged at him was as persistent as the buzz in his earphones. And an idea came. If he *were* obeying some strange call for assistance, couldn't that in some way lead him to what he sought? The only difficulty was that he had no way of being more receptive to the impulse than he now was. He could not use it as a compass bearing.

In the end he chose the Center as his goal, reasoning that if the prisoner were to be interviewed by the leaders of the aliens, he would be taken to those rulers, they would not go to him. From a concealed place across from the open square on which the building fronted, the pilot studied it carefully. It towered several stories above the surrounding structures, to some of which it was tied by the ways above the streets. To use one of those bridges as a means of entering the headquarters would be entirely too conspicuous.

As far as the pilot was able to judge, there was only one entrance on the ground level, the wide front door with the imposing picture-covered gates. Had he had free use of the flitter he might have tried to swing down from the hovering machine after dark. But he was sure that Captain Hobart would not welcome the suggestion.

Underground? There had been those ways in that other city, a city which, though built on a much smaller scale, was not too different in general outline from this one. The idea was worth investigation.

The doorway, which had afforded him a shelter from which to spy out the land, yielded to his push, and he went through three large rooms on the ground floor, paying no attention to the strange groups of furnishings, but seeking something else, which he had luck to find in the last room, a ramp leading down.

It was in the underground that he made his first important find. They had seen ground vehicles in the city, a few still in operation, but Raf had gathered that the fuel and extra parts for the machines were now so scarce that they were only used in emergencies. Here, however, was a means of transportation quite different, a tunnel through which ran a ribbon of belt, wide enough to accommodate three or four passengers at once. It did not move, but when Raf dared to step out upon its surface, it swung under his weight. Since it ran in the general direction of the Center he decided to use it. It trembled under his tread, but he found that he could run along it making no sound.

The tunnel was not in darkness, for square plates set in the roof gave a diffused violet light. However, not too far ahead, the light was brighter, and it came from one side, not the roof. Another station on this abandoned way? The pilot approached it with caution. If his bump of direction was not altogether off, this must be either below the Center or very close to it.

The second station proved to be a junction where more than one of the elastic paths met. Though he crouched to listen for a long moment before venturing out into that open space, he could hear or see nothing which suggested that the aliens ever came down now to these levels.

They had provided an upward ramp, and Raf climbed it, only to meet his first defeat at its top. For here was no opening to admit him to the ground floor of what he hoped was the Center. Baffled by the smooth surface over which he vainly ran his hands seeking for some clue to the door, he decided that the aliens had, for some purpose of their own, walled off the lower regions. Discouraged, he returned to the junction level. But he was not content to surrender his plans so easily. Slowly he made a circuit of the platform, examining the walls and celling. He found an air shaft, a wide opening striking up into the heart of the building above.

It was covered with a grille and it was above his reach but....

Raf measured distances and planned his effort. The mouth of a junction tunnel ran less than two feet away from that grille. The opening was outlined with a ledge, which made a complete arch from the floor. He stopped and triggered the gravity plates in his space boots. Made to give freedom of action when the ship was in free fall, they might just provide a weak suction here. And they did! He was able to climb that arch and, standing on it, work loose the grille which had been fashioned to open. Now....

The pilot flashed his hand torch up into that dark well. He had been right—and lucky! There were holds at regular intervals, something must have been serviced by workmen in here. This was going to be easy. His fingers found the first hold, and he wormed his way into the shaft.

It was not a difficult climb, for there were niches along the way where the alien mechanics who had once made repairs had either rested or done some of their work. And there were also grilles on each level which gave him at least a partial view of what lay beyond.

His guess was right; he recognized the main hall of the Center as he climbed past the grid there, heading up toward those levels where he was sure the leaders of the aliens had their private quarters. Twice he paused to look in upon conferences of the gaudily wrapped and painted civilians, but, since he could not understand what they were saying, it was a waste of time to linger.

He was some eight floors up when chance, luck, or that mysterious something which had brought him into this venture, led him to the right place at the right time. There was one of those niches, and he had just settled into it, peering out through the grid, when he saw the door at the opposite end of the room open and in marched a party of warriors with a prisoner in their midst.

Raf's eyes went wide. It was the captive he sought; he had no doubt of that. But who—what—was that prisoner?

This was no fur-covered half-animal, nor was it one of the delicate-boned, decadent, painted creatures such as those who now ringed in their captive. Though the man had been roughly handled and now reeled rather than walked, Raf thought for one wild instant that it was one of the crew from the spacer. The light hair, showing rings of curl, the tanned face which, beneath dirt and bruises, displayed a very familiar cast of features, the body hardly covered by rags of clothing—they were all so like those of his own kind that his mind at first refused to believe that this was *not* someone he knew. Yet as the party moved toward his hiding place he knew that he was facing a total stranger.

Stranger or no, Raf was sure that he saw a Terran. Had another ship made a landing on this planet? One of those earlier ships whose fate had been a mystery on their home world? Who—and when—and why? He huddled as close to the grid as he could get, alert to the slightest movement below as the prisoner faced his captors.

15

ARENA

The dull pain which throbbed through Dalgard's skull with every beat of his heart was confusing, and it was hard to think clearly. But the colony scout, soon after he had fought his way back to consciousness, had learned that he was imprisoned somewhere in the globe ship. Just as he now knew that he had been brought across the sea from the continent on which Homeport was situated and that he had no hope of rescue.

He had seen little of his captors, and the guards, who had hustled him from one place of imprisonment to another, had not spoken to him, nor had he tried to communicate with them. At first he had been too sick and confused, then too wary. These were clearly Those Others and the conditioning which had surrounded him from birth had instilled in him a deep distrust of the former masters of Astra.

Now Dalgard was more alert, and his being brought to this room in what was certainly the center of the alien civilization made him believe that he was about to meet the rulers of the enemy. So he stared curiously about him as the guards jostled him through the door.

On a dais fashioned of heaped-up rainbow-colored pads were three aliens, their legs folded under them at what seemed impossible angles. One wore the black wrappings, the breastplate of the guards, but the other two had indulged their love of color in weird, eye-disturbing combinations of shades in the bandages wrapping the thin limbs and paunchy bodies. They were, as far as he could see through the thick layers of paint overlaying their skins, older than their officer companion. But nothing in their attitude suggested that age had mellowed them.

Dalgard was brought to stand before the trio as before a tribunal of judges. His sword-knife had been taken from his belt before he had regained his senses, his hands were twisted behind his back and locked together in a bar and hoop arrangement. He certainly could offer little threat to the company, yet they ringed him in, weapons ready, watching his every move. The scout licked cracked lips. There was one thing they could not control, could not prevent him from doing. Somewhere, not too far away, was help ...

Not from the merpeople, but he was sure that he had been in contact with another friendly mind. Since the hour of his awakening on board the globe ship, when he had half-consciously sent out an appeal for aid over the band which united him with Sssuri's race, and had touched that other consciousness—not the cold alien stream about him—he had been sure that somewhere within the enemy throng there was a potential savior. Was it among those who manned the strange flyer, those the merpeople had spied upon but whom he had not yet seen?

Dalgard had striven since that moment of contact to keep in touch with the nebulous other mind, to project his need for help. But he had been unable to enter in freely as he could with his own kind, or with Sssuri and the sea people. Now, even as he stood in the heart of the enemy territory completely at the mercy of the aliens, he felt, more strongly than ever before, that another, whose mind he could not enter and yet who was in some queer way sensitive to his appeal, was close at hand. He searched the painted faces before him trying to probe behind each locked mask, but he was certain that the one he sought was not there. Only—he must be! The contact was so strong—Dalgard's startled eyes went to the wall behind the dais, tried vainly to trace what could only be felt. He would be willing to give a knife oath that the stranger was within seeing, listening distance at this minute!

While he was so engrossed in his own problem, the guard had moved. The hooped bar which locked his wrists was loosened, and his arms, each tight in the grip of one of the warriors were brought out before him. The officer on the dais tossed a metal ring to one of the guards.

Roughly the warrior holding Dalgard's left arm forced the band over his hand and jerked it up his forearm as far as it would go. As it winked in the light the scout was reminded of a similar bracelet he had seen—where? On the front leg of the snake-devil he had shot!

The officer produced a second ring, slipping it smoothly over his own arm, adjusting it to touch bare skin and not the wrappings which served him as a sleeve. Dalgard thought he understood. A device to facilitate communication. And straightway he was wary. When his ancestors had first met the merpeople, they had established a means of speech through touch, the palm of one resting against the palm of the other. In later generations, when they had developed their new senses, physical contact had not been necessary. However, here—Dalgard's eyes narrowed, the line along his jaw was hard.

He had always accepted the merpeople's estimate of Those Others, that their ancient enemies were all-seeing and all-knowing, with mental powers far beyond their own definition or description. Now he half expected to be ruthlessly mind-invaded, stripped of everything the enemy desired to know.

So he was astonished when the words which formed in his thoughts were simple, almost childish. And while he prepared to answer them, another part of him watched and listened, waiting for the attack he was sure would come.

"You—are—who—what?"

He forced a look of astonishment. Nor did he make the mistake of answering that mentally. If Those Others did not know he could use the mind speech, why betray his power?

"I am of the stars," he answered slowly, aloud, using the speech of Homeport. He had so little occasion to talk lately that his voice sounded curiously rusty and harsh in his own ears. Nor had he the least idea of the impression those few archaically accented words would have on one who heard them.

To Dalgard's inner surprise the answer did not astonish his interrogator. The alien officer might well have been expecting to hear just that. But he pulled off his own arm band before he turned to his fellows with a spurt of the twittering speech they used among themselves. While the two civilians were still trilling, the officer edged forward an inch or so and stared at Dalgard intently as he replaced the band.

"You not look—same—as others—"

"I do not know what you mean. Here are not others like me."

One of the civilians twitched at the officer's sleeve, apparently demanding a translation, but the other shook him off impatiently.

"You come from sky—now?"

Dalgard shook his head, then realized that gesture might not mean anything to his audience. "Long ago before I was, my people came."

The alien digested that, then again took off his band before he relayed it to his companions. The excited twitter of their speech scaled up.

"You travel with the beasts—" the alien's accusation came crisply while the others gabbled. "That which hunts could not have tracked you had not the stink of the beast things been on you."

"I know no beasts," Dalgard faced up to that squarely. "The sea people are my friends!"

It was hard to read any emotion on these lacquered and bedaubed faces, but before the officer once more broke bracelet contact, Dalgard did sense the other's almost hysterical aversion. The scout might just have admitted to the most revolting practices as far as the alien was concerned. After he had translated, all three of those on the dais were silent. Even the guards edged away from the captive as if in some manner they might be defiled by proximity. One of the civilians made an emphatic statement, got creakily to his feet, and walked always as if he would have nothing more to do with this matter. After a second or two of hesitation his fellow followed his example.

The officer turned the bracelet around in his fingers, his dark eyes with their slitted pupils never leaving Dalgard's face. Then he came to a decision. He pushed the ring up his arm, and the words which reached the prisoner were coldly remote, as if the captive were no longer judged an intelligent living creature but something which had no right of existence in a well-ordered universe.

"Beast friends with beast. As the beasts—so shall you end. It is spoken."

One of the guards tore the bracelet from Dalgard's arm, trying not to touch the scout's flesh in the process. And those who once more shackled his wrists ostentatiously wiped their hands up and down the wrappings on their thighs afterwards.

But before they jabbed him into movement with the muzzles of their weapons, Dalgard located at last the source of that disturbing mental touch, not only located it, but in some manner broke through the existing barrier between the strange mind and his and communicated as clearly with it as he might have with Sssuri. And the excitement of his discovery almost led to self-betrayal!

Terran! One of those who traveled with the aliens? Yet he read clearly the other's distrust of that company, the fact that he lay in concealment here without their knowledge. And he was not unfriendly—surely he could not be a Peaceman of Pax! Another fugitive from a newly-come colony ship—? Dalgard beamed a warning to the other. If he who was free could only reach the merpeople! It might mean the turning point in their whole venture!

Dalgard was furiously planning, simplifying, trying to impress the most imperative message on that other mind as he stumbled away in the midst of the guards. The stranger was

Andre Norton

confused, apparently Dalgard's arrival, his use of the mind touch, had been an overwhelming surprise. But if he could only make the right move—would make it—The scout from Homeport had no idea what was in store for him, but with one of his own breed here and suspicious of the aliens he had at least a slim chance. He snapped the thread of communication. Now he must be ready for any opportunity—

Raf watched that amazing apparition go out of the room below. He was shaking with a chill born of no outside cold. First the shock of hearing that language, queerly accented as the words were, then that sharp contact, mind to mind. He was being clearly warned against revealing himself. The stranger was a Terran, Raf would swear to that. So somewhere on this world there was a Terran colony! One of those legendary ships of outlaws, who had taken to space during the rule of Pax, had made the crossing safely and had here established a foothold.

While one part of Raf's brain fitted together the jigsaw of bits and patches of information, the other section dealt with that message of warning the other had beamed to him. The pilot knew that the captive must be in immediate danger. He could not understand all that had happened in that interview with the aliens, but he was left with the impression that the prisoner had been not only tried but condemned. And it was up to him to help.

But how? By the time he got back to the flitter or was able to find Hobart and the others, it might already be too late. *He* must make the move, and soon, for there had been unmistakable urgency in the captive's message. Raf's hands fumbled at the grid before him, and then he realized that the opening was far too small to admit him to the room on the other side of the wall.

To return to the underground ways might be a waste of time, but he could see no other course open to him. What if he could not find the captive later? Where in the maze of the half-deserted city could he hope to come across the trail again? Even as he sorted out all the points which could defeat him, Raf's hands and feet felt for the notched steps which would take him down. He had gone only two floors when he was faced with a grille opening which was much larger. On impulse he stopped to measure it, sure he could squeeze through here, if he could work loose the grid.

Prying with one hand and a tool from his belt pouch, he struggled not only against the stubborn metal but against time. That strange mental communication had ceased. Though he was sure that he still received a trace of it from time to time, just enough to reassure him that the prisoner was still alive. And each time it touched him Raf redoubled his efforts on the metal clasps of the grid. At last his determination triumphed, and the grille swung out, to fall with an appalling clatter to the floor.

The pilot thrust his feet through the opening and wriggled desperately, expecting any moment to confront a reception committee drawn by the noise. But when he reached the floor, the hallway was still vacant. In fact, he was conscious of a hush in the whole building, as if those who made their homes within its walls were elsewhere. That silence acted on him as a spur.

Raf ran along the corridor, trying to subdue the clatter of his space boots, coming to a downward ramp. There he paused, unable to decide whether to go down—until he caught sight of a party of aliens below, walking swiftly enough to suggest that they too were in a hurry.

This small group was apparently on its way to some

gathering. And in it for the first time the Terran saw the women of the aliens, or at least the fully veiled, gliding creatures he guessed were the females of the painted people. There were four of them in the group ahead, escorted by two of the males, and the high fluting of their voices resounded along the corridor as might the cheeping of birds. If the males were colorful in their choice of body wrappings, the females were gorgeous beyond belief, as cloudy stuff which had the changing hues of Terran opals frothed about them to completely conceal their figures.

The harsher twittering of the men had an impatient note, and the whole party quickened pace until their glide was close to an undignified trot. Raf, forced to keep well behind lest his boots betray him, fumed.

They did not go into the open, but took another way which sloped down once more. Luckily the journey was not a long one. Ahead was light which suggested the outdoors.

Raf sucked in his breath as he came out a goodly distance behind the aliens. Established in what was once a court surrounded by the towers and buildings of the city was a miniature of that other arena where he had seen the dead lizard things. The glittering, gayly dressed aliens were taking their places on the tiers of seats. But the place which had been built to accommodate at least a thousand spectators now housed less than half the number. If this was the extent of the alien nation, it was the dregs of a dwindling race.

Directly below where Raf lingered in an aisle dividing the tiers of seats, there was a manhole opening with a barred gate across it, an entrance to the sand-covered enclosure. And fortunately the aliens were all clustered close to the oval far from that spot.

Also the attention of the audience was firmly riveted on events below. A door at the sand level had been flung open, and through it was now hustled the prisoner. Either the aliens still possessed some idea of fair play or they hoped to prolong a contest to satisfy their own pleasure, for the captive's hands were unbound and he clutched a spear.

Remembering far-off legends of earlier and more savage civilizations on his own world, Raf was now sure that the lone man below was about to fight for his life. The question was, against what?

Another of the mouthlike openings around the edge of the arena opened, and one of the furry people shambled out, weaving weakly from side to side as he came, a spear in his scaled paws. He halted a step or two into the open, his round head swinging from side to side, spittle drooling from his gaping mouth. His body was covered with raw sores and bare patches from which the fur had been torn away, and it was apparent that he had long been the victim of ill-usage, if not torture.

Shrill cries arose from the alien spectators as the furred one blinked in the light and then sighted the man some feet away. He stiffened, his arm drew back, the spear poised. Then as suddenly it dropped to his side, and he fell on his knees before wriggling across the sand, his paws held out imploringly to his fellow captive.

The cries from the watching aliens were threatening. Several rose in their seats gesturing to the two below. And Raf, thankful for their absorption, sped down to the manhole, discovering to his delight it could be readily opened from his side. As he edged it around, there was another sound below. This was no high-pitched fluting from aliens deprived of their sport, but a hissing nightmare cry.

Raf's line of vision, limited by the door, framed a portion of scaled back, as it looked, immediately below him. His hand went to the blast bombs as he descended the runway, and his boots hit the sand just as the drama below reached its climax.

The furred one lay prone in the sand, uncaring. Above that mistreated body, the human stood in the half-crouch of a fighting man, the puny spear pointed up bravely at a mark it could not hope to reach, the soft throat of one of the giant lizards. The reptile did not move to speedily destroy. Instead, hissing, it reared above the two as if studying them with a vicious intelligence. But there was no time to wonder how long it would delay striking.

Raf's strong teeth ripped loose the tag end of the blast bomb, and he lobbed it straight with a practiced arm so that the ball spiraled across the arena to come to rest between the massive hind legs of the lizard. He saw the man's eyes widen as they fastened on him. And then the human captive flung himself to the earth, half covering the body of the furred one. The reptile grabbed in the same instant, its grasping claws cutting only air, and before it could try a second time the bomb went off.

Literally torn apart by the explosion, the creature must have died at once. But the captive moved. He was on his feet again, pulling his companion up with him, before the startled spectators could guess what had happened. Then half carrying the other prisoner, he ran, not onward to the waiting Raf, but for the gate through which he had come into the arena. At the same time a message beat into the Terran's brain—

"This way!"

Avoiding bits of horrible refuse, Raf obeyed that order, catching up in a couple of strides with the other two and linking his arm through the dangling one of the furred creature to take some of the strain from the stranger.

"Have you any more of the power things?" the words came in the archaic speech of his own world.

"Two more bombs," he answered.

"We may have to blow the gate here," the other panted breathlessly.

Instead Raf drew his stun gun. The gate was already opening, a wedge of the painted warriors heading through, flame-throwers ready. He sprayed wide, and on the highest level. A spout of fire singed the cloth of his tunic across the top of his shoulder as one of the last aliens fired before his legs buckled and he went down. Then, opposition momentarily gone, the two with their semiconscious charge stumbled over the bodies of the guards and reached the corridor beyond.

16

SURPRISE ATTACK

So much had happened so quickly during the past hour that Dalgard had no chance to plan or even sort out impressions in his mind. He had no guess as to where this stranger, now taking some of the burden of the wounded merman from him, had sprung from. The other's clothing, the helmet covering his head were more akin to those worn by the aliens than they were to the dress of the colonist. Yet the man beneath those trappings was of the same breed as his own people. And he could not believe he was a Peaceman of Pax—all he had done here spoke against those legends of dark Terran days Dalgard had heard from childhood. But where had he come from? The only answer could be another outlaw colony ship.

"We are in the inner ways," Dalgard tried to reach the mind of the merman as they pounded on into the corridors which led from the arena. "Do you know these—" He had a faint hope that the sea man because of his longer captivity might have a route of escape to suggest.

"—down to the lower levels—" the thought came slowly, forced out by a weakening will. "Lower—levels—roads to the sea—"

That was what Dalgard had been hoping for, some passage which would run seaward and so to safety, such as he had found with Sssuri in that other city.

"What are we hunting?" the stranger broke in, and Dalgard realized that perhaps the other did not follow the mind talk. His words had an odd inflection, a clipped accent which was new.

"A lower way," he returned in the speech of his own people.

"To the right." The merman, struggling against his own weakness, had raised his head and was looking about as one who searches for a familiar landmark.

There was a branching way to the right, and Dalgard swung into it, bringing the other two after him. This was a narrow passage, and twice they brushed by sealed doors. It brought them up against a blank wall. The stranger wheeled, his odd weapon ready, for they could hear the shouts of pursuers behind them. But the merman pulled free of Dalgard and went down on the floor to dig with his taloned fingers at some depressions there.

"Open here," the thought came clearly, "then down!"

Dalgard went down on one knee, able now to see the outline of a trap door. It must be pried up. His sword-knife was gone, the spear they had given him for the arena he had dropped when he dragged the merman out of danger. He looked to the stranger. About the other's narrow hips was slung a belt from which hung pouches and tools the primitive colonist could not evaluate. But there was also a bush knife, and he reached for it.

"The knife—"

The stranger glanced down at the blade he wore in surprise, as if he had forgotten it. Then with one swift movement he drew it from its sheath and flipped it to Dalgard.

On the track behind the clamor was growing, and the colony scout worked with concentration at his task of fitting the blade into the crack and freeing the door. As soon as there was space enough, the merman's claws recklessly slid under, and he added what strength he could to Dalgard's. The door arose and fell back onto the pavement with a clang, exposing a dark pit.

"Got 'em!" the words burst from the stranger. He had pressed the firing button of his weapon. Where the passage in which they stood met the main corridor, there was an agitated shouting and then sudden silence.

"Down—" The merman had crawled to the edge of the opening. From it rose a dank, fetid smell. Now that the noise in the corridor was stilled Dalgard could hear something: the sound of water.

"How do we get down?" he questioned the merman.

"It is far, there are no climbing holds—"

Dalgard straightened. Well, he supposed, even a leap into that was better than to be taken a second time by Those Others. But was he ready for such a desperate solution?

"A long way down?" The stranger leaned over to peer into the well.

"He says so," Dalgard nodded at the merman. "And there are no climbing holds."

The stranger plucked at the front of his tunic with one hand, still holding his weapon with the other. From an opening he drew a line, and Dalgard grabbed it eagerly, testing the first foot with a sharp jerk. He had never seen such stuff, so light of weight and yet so tough. His delight reached the merman, who sat up to gaze owlishly at the coils the stranger pulled from concealment.

They used the door of the well for the lowering beam, hitching the cord about it. Then the merman noosed one end about him, and Dalgard, the door taking some of the strain, lowered him. The end of the cord was perilously close to the scout's fingers when there was a signaling pull from below, and he was free to reel in the loose line. He turned to the stranger.

"You go. I'll watch them." The other waved his weapon to the corridor.

There was some sense to that, Dalgard had to agree. He made fast the end of the cord and went in his turn into the dark, burning the palm of one hand before he was able to slacken the speed of his descent. Then he landed thigh-deep in water, from which arose an unpleasant smell.

"All right—Come—" he put full force into the thought he beamed at the stranger above. When the other did not obey, Dalgard began to wonder if he should climb to his aid. Had the aliens broken through and overwhelmed the other? Or what had happened? The rope whisked up out of his hands. And a moment later a voice rang eerily overhead.

"Clear below! Coming down!"

Dalgard scrambled out of the space under the opening, heading on into the murk where the merman waited. There was a splash as the stranger hit the stream, and the rope lashed down behind him at their united jerk.

"Where do we go from here?" The voice carried through the dark.

Scaled fingers hooked about Dalgard's right hand and tugged him on. He reached back in turn and locked grip with the stranger. So united the three splashed on through the rancid liquid. In time they came out of the first tunnel into a wider section, but here the odor was worse, catching in their throats, making them sway dizzily. There seemed to be no end to these ways, which Raf guessed were the drains of the ancient city.

Only the merman appeared to have a definite idea of where they were going, though he halted once or twice when they came to a side passage as if thinking out their course. Since the man from the arena accepted the furred one's guidance, Raf depended upon it too. Though he wondered if they would ever find their way out into the open once more.

He was startled by sudden pain as the hand leading him tightened its grip to bone-bruising force. They had stopped, and the liquid washed about them until Raf wondered if he would ever feel clean again. When they started on, they moved much more swiftly. His companions were in a hurry, but Raf was unprepared for the sight which broke as they came out in a high-roofed cavern.

There was an odd, cold light there—but that light was not all he saw. Drawn up on a ledge rising out of the contaminated stream were rows of the furred people, all sitting in silence, bone spears resting across their knees, long knives at their belts. They watched with round, unblinking eyes the three who had just come out of the side passage. The rescued merman loosened his grip on Dalgard's hand and waded forward to confront that quiet, waiting assembly. Neither he nor his fellows made any sound, and Raf guessed that they had some other form of communication, perhaps the same telepathic ability to broadcast messages which this amazing man beside him displayed.

"They are of his tribe," the other explained, sensing that Raf could not understand. "They came here to try to save him, for he is one of their Speakers-for-Many."

"Who are they? Who are you?" Raf asked the two questions which had been with him ever since the wild adventure had begun.

"They are the People-of-the-Sea, our friends, our knife brothers. And I am of Homeport. My people came from the stars in a ship, but not a ship of this world. We have been here for many years."

The mermen were moving now. Several had waded forward to greet their chief, aiding him ashore. But when Raf moved toward the ledge, Dalgard put out a restraining hand.

"Until we are summoned—no. They have their customs. And this is a party-for-war. This tribe knows not my people, save by rumor. We wait."

Raf looked over the ranks of the sea folk. The light came from globes borne by every twentieth warrior, a globe in which something that gave off phosphorescent gleams swam around and around. The spears which each merman carried were slender and wickedly barbed, the knives almost sword length. The pilot remembered the flame-throwers of the aliens and could not see any victory for the merman party.

"No, knife blade against the fire—that is not equal."

Raf started, amazed and then irritated that the other had read his thoughts so easily.

"But what else can be done? Some stand must be taken, even if a whole tribe goes down to the Great Dark because they do it."

"What do you mean?" Raf demanded.

"Is it not the truth that Those Others went across the sea to plunder their forgotten storehouse of knowledge?" countered the other. He spoke slowly as if he found difficulty in clothing thoughts with words. "Sssuri said that was why they came."

Raf, remembering what he had seen—the stripping of shelves and tables of the devices that were stored on them—could only nod.

"Then it is also true that soon they will have worse than fire with which to hunt us down. And they shall turn against your colony as they will against Homeport. For the mermen, and their own records, have taught us that it is their nature to rule, that they can live in peace only when all living things on this world are their slaves."

"My colony?" Raf was momentarily diverted. "I'm one of a spacer's crew, not the member of any colony!"

Dalgard stared at the stranger. His guess had been right. A new ship, another ship which had recently crossed deep space to find them had flown the dark wastes even as the First Elders had done! It must be that more outlaws had come to find a new home! This was wonderful news, news he must take to Homeport. Only, it was news which must wait. For the sea people had come to a decision of their own.

"What are they going to do now?" Raf asked.

The mermen were not retreating, instead they were slipping from the ledge in regular order, forming somewhat crooked ranks in the water.

Dalgard did not reply at once, making mind touch not only to ask but to impress his kinship on the sea people. They were united in a single-minded purpose, with failure before them—unless—He turned to the stranger.

"They go to war upon Those Others. He who guided us here knows also that the new knowledge they have brought into the city is danger. If an end is not put to it before they can use it, then"—he shrugged—"the mermen must retreat into the depths. And we, who can not follow them—" He made a quick, thrusting gesture as if using a knife on his own throat. "For a time Those Others have been growing fewer in number and weaker. Their children are not many and sometimes there are years when none are born at all. And they have forgotten so much. But now, perhaps they can increase once more, not only in wisdom and strength of arms, but in numbers. The mermen have kept a watch on them, content to let matters rest, sure that time would defeat them. But now, time no longer fights on our side."

Raf watched the furred people with their short spears, their knives. He recalled that rocky island where the aliens had unleashed the fire. The expeditionary force would not have a chance against that.

"But *your* weapons would." The words addressed to him were clear, though they had not been spoken aloud. Raf's hand went to the pocket where two more of the blast bombs rested. "And this is your battle as much as ours!"

But it wasn't his fight! Dalgard had gone too far with that suggestion. Raf had no ties on this world, the *RS 10* was waiting to take him away. It was strictly against all orders, all his training, for him to become involved in alien warfare. The pilot's hand went back to his belt. He was not going to allow himself to be pushed onto anything foolish, whether this "colonist" could read his mind or not.

The first ranks of the mermen had already waded past them, heading into the way down which the escaping prisoners had come. To Raf's eyes none of them paid any attention to the two humans as they went, though they were probably in mental touch with his companion.

"You are already termed one of us in *their* eyes," Dalgard was careful to use oral speech this time. "When you came to our rescue in the arena they believed that you were of our kind. Do you think you can return to walk safely through the city? So"—he drew a hissing breath of surprise when the thought which leaped into Raf's mind was plain to Dalgard also—"you have—there are more of you there! But already Those Others may be moving against them because of what you have done!"

Raf who had been about to join the mermen stopped short. That aspect had not struck him before. What had happened to Soriki and the flitter, to the captain and Lablet, who had been in the heart of the enemy territory when he had challenged the aliens? It would be only logical that the painted people would consider them all dangerous now. He must get out of here, back to the flitter, try to help where unwittingly he had harmed—

Dalgard caught up with him. He had been able to read a little of what had passed through the other's mind. Though it was difficult to sort order out of the tangled thoughts. The longer he was with the stranger, the more aware he became of the differences between them. Outwardly they might appear of the same species, but inwardly—Dalgard frowned—there was something that he must consider later, when they had a thinking space. But now he could understand the other's agitation. It was very true that Those Others might turn on the stranger's fellows in retaliation for his deeds.

Together they joined the mermen. There was no talk, nothing to break the splashing sound of bodies moving against the current. As they pressed on, Raf was sure that this was not the same way they had come. And once more Dalgard answered his unspoken question.

"We seek another door into the city, one long known to these tribesmen."

Raf would gladly have run, but he could not move faster than his guides, and while their pace seemed deliberate, they did not pause to rest. The whole city, he decided, must be honeycombed with these drains. After traversing a fourth tunnel, they climbed out of the flood onto a dry passage, which wormed along, almost turning on itself at times.

Side passages ran out from this corridor like rootlets from a parent root, and small parties of mermen broke from the regiment to follow certain ones, leaving without orders or farewells. At the fifth of these Dalgard touched Raf's arm and drew him aside.

"This is our way." Tensely the scout waited. If the stranger refused, then the one plan the scout had formed during the past half-hour would fail. He still held to the hope that Raf, with what Raf carried, could succeed in the only project which would mean, perhaps not his safety nor the safety of the tribe he now marched among, but the eventual safety of Astra itself, the safety of all the harmless people of the sea, the little creatures of the grass and the sky, of his own land at Homeport. He would have to force Raf into action if need be. He did not use the mind touch; he knew now the unspoken resentment which followed that. If it became necessary— Dalgard's hands balled into fists—he would strike down the stranger—take from him—Swiftly he turned his thoughts from that. It might be easy, now that he had established mental contact with this off-worlder, for the other to pick up a thought as vivid as that.

But luckily Raf obediently turned into the side passage with the six mermen who were to attack at this particular point. The way grew narrower until they crept on hands and knees between rough walls which were not of the same construction as the larger tunnels. The smaller mermen had no difficulty in getting through, but twice Raf's equipment belt caught on projections and he had to fight his way free.

They crawled one by one into a ventilation shaft much like the one he had climbed at the Center. Dalgard's whisper reached him.

"We are now in the building which houses their sky ship."

"I know that one," Raf returned almost eagerly, glad at last to be back so close to familiar territory. He climbed up the hand-and footholds the sea-monster lamp disclosed, wishing the mermen ahead would speed up.

The grille at the head of the shaft had been removed, and the invaders arose one by one into a dim and dusty place of motionless machinery, which, by all tangible evidence, had not been entered for some time. But the cautious manner in which the sea people strung out to approach the far door argued that the same might not be true beyond.

For the first time Raf noticed that his human companion now held one of the knives of the merpeople, and he drew his stun gun. But he could not forget the flame-throwers which might at that very moment be trained upon the other side of that door by the aliens. They might be walking into a trap.

He half expected one of those disconcerting thought answers from Dalgard. But the scout was playing safe—nothing must upset the stranger. Confronted by what had to be done, he might be influenced into acting for them. So Dalgard strode softly ahead, apparently not interested in Raf.

One of the mermen worked at the door, using the point of his spear as a lever. Here again was a vista of machinery. But these machines were alive; a faint hum came from their casings. The mermen scattered, taking cover, a move copied by the two humans.

The pilot remained in hiding, but he saw one of the furred people running on as light-footedly as a shadow. Then his arm drew back, and he cast his spear. Raf fancied he could hear a faint whistle as the weapon cut the air. There was a cry, and the merman ran on, vanishing into the shadows, to return a second or two later wiping stains from his weapon. Out of their places of concealment, his fellows gathered about him. And the humans followed.

Now they were fronted by a ramp leading up, and the mermen took it quickly, their bare, scaled feet setting up a whispering echo which was drowned by the clop of Raf's boots. Once more the party was alert, ready for trouble, and taking his cue from them, he kept his stun gun in his hand.

Andre Norton

But the maneuver at the head of the ramp surprised him. For, though he had heard no signal, all the party but one plastered their bodies back against the wall, Dalgard pulling Raf into position beside him, the scout's muscular bare arm pinning the pilot into a narrow space. One merman stood at the crack of the door at the top of the ramp. He pushed the barrier open and crept in.

Meanwhile those who waited poised their spears, all aimed at that door. Raf fingered the button on his gun to "spray" as he had when he had faced the attack of the scavengers in the arena tunnels.

There was a cry, a shout with a summons in it. And the venturesome merman thudded back through the door. But he was not alone. Two of the black guardsmen, their flamers spitting fiery death, ran behind him, and the curling lash of one of those flames almost wreathed the runner before he swung aside. Raf fired without consciously aiming. Both of the sentries fell forward, to slide limply down the ramp.

Then Dalgard pulled him on. "The way is open," he said. "This is it!" There was an excited exultation in his voice.

17

DESTRUCTION UNLEASHED

The space they now entered must be the core of the building, Raf thought a little dazedly. For there, towering over them was the round bulb of the globe. And about its open hatch were piles of the material which he had last seen in the warehouse on the other continent. The unloading of the alien ship had been hastily interrupted.

Since neither the merman nor Dalgard took cover, Raf judged that they did not fear attack now. But when he turned his attention away from the ship, he found not only the colony scout but most of the sea people gathered about him as if waiting for some action on his part.

"What is it?" He could feel it, that strong pressure, that band united, in willing him into some move. His stubborn streak of independence made his reaction contrary. He was not going to be pushed into anything.

"In this hour," Dalgard spoke aloud, avoiding the mind touch which might stiffen Raf's rebellion. He wished that some older, wiser Elder from Homeport were there. So little time—Yet this stranger with practically no effort might accomplish all they had come to do, if he could only be persuaded into action. "In this hour, here is the heart of what civilization remains to Those Others. Destroy it, and it will not matter whether they kill us. For in the days to come they will have nothing left."

Raf understood. This was why he had been brought here. They wanted him to use the blast bombs. And one part of him *was* calculating the best places to set his two remaining bombs for the wildest possible destruction. That part of him could accept the logic of Dalgard's reasoning. He doubted if the aliens could repair the globe if it were damaged, and he was sure that much which they had brought back from the eastern continent was irreplaceable. The bombs had not been intended for such a use. They were defensive, anti-personal weapons to be employed as he had done against the lizard in the arena. But placed properly—Without thinking his hands went to the sealed pocket in the breast of his tunic.

Dalgard saw that gesture and inside him some taut cord began to unwind. Then the stranger's hands dropped, and he swung around to face the colony scout squarely, a scowl twisting his black brows almost together.

"This isn't my fight," he stated flatly. "I've got to get back to the flitter, to my spacer—"

What was the matter? Dalgard tried to understand. If the aliens won now, this stranger was in as great a danger as were the rest of them. Did he believe that Those Others would allow any colony to be established on a world they ruled?

"There will be no future for you here," he spoke slowly, trying with all his power to get through to the other. "They will not allow you to found another Homeport. You will have no colony—"

"Will you get it into your thick head," burst out the pilot, "that I'm not here to start a colony! We can take off from this blasted planet whenever we want to. We didn't come here to stay!"

Beneath the suntan, Dalgard's face whitened. The other had come from no outlaw ship, seeking a refuge across space, as his own people had fled to a new life from tyranny. His first fears had been correct! This was a representative of Pax, doubtless sent to hunt down the descendants of those who had escaped its throttling dictatorship. The slender strangely garbed Terran might be of the same blood as his own, but he was as great an enemy as Those Others!

"Pax!" He did not know that he had said that word aloud.

The other laughed. "You are living back in history. Pax has been dead and gone almost two centuries. I'm of the Federation of Free Men—"

"Will the stranger use his fire now?" The question formed in Dalgard's mind. The mermen were growing impatient, as well they might. This was no time for talk, but for action. Could Raf be persuaded to aid them? A Federation of Free Men—Free Men! That was what they were fighting for here and now.

"You are free," he said. "The sea people won their freedom when Those Others fought among themselves. My people came across the star void in search of freedom, paying in blood to win it. But these, these are not the weapons of the free." He pointed to the supplies about the globe, to the globe itself.

The mermen were waiting no longer. With the butts of their spears they smashed anything breakable. But the damage one

could do by hand in the short space of time granted them—
Raf was surprised that a guard was not already down upon
them—was sharply limited. The piled-up secrets of an old
race, a race which had once ruled a planet. He thought
fleetingly of Lablet's preoccupation with this spoil, of
Hobart's hope of gaining knowledge they could take back
with them. But would the aliens keep their part of the
bargain? He no longer believed that.

Why not give these barbarians a chance, and the colonists.
Sure, he was breaking the stiffest rule of the Service. But,
perhaps by now the flitter was gone, he might never reach
the *RS 10*. It was not his war, right enough. But he'd give the
weaker side a fighting chance.

Dalgard followed him into the globe ship, climbing the
ladders to the engine level, watching with curious eyes as
Raf inspected the driving power of the ship and made the
best disposition possible of one of the bombs.

Then they were on the ladder once more as the ship shook
under them, plates buckling as a great wound tore three
decks apart. Raf laughed recklessly. Now that he was
committed to this course, he had a small-boy delight in the
destruction.

"They won't raise her again in a hurry," he confided to
Dalgard. But the other did not share his triumph.

"They come—we must move fast," the scout urged.

When they jumped from the hatch, they discovered that the
mermen had been busy in their turn. As many of the supplies
as they could move had been pushed and piled into one great
mass. Broken crystal littered the floor in shards and puddles of
strange chemicals mingled smells to become a throat-rasping

fog. Raf eyed those doubtfully. Some of those fumes might combine in the blast—

Once again Dalgard read his mind and waved the mermen back, sending them through the door to the ramp and the lower engine room. Raf stood in the doorway, the bomb in his hand, knowing that it was time for him to make the most accurate cast of his life.

The sphere left his fingers, was a gleam in the murky air. It struck the pile of material. Then the whole world was hidden by a blinding glare.

It was dark—black dark. And he was swinging back and forth through this total darkness. He was a ball, a blast bomb being tossed from hand to hand through the dark by painted warriors who laughed shrilly at his pain, tossed through the dark. Fear such as he had never known, even under the last acceleration pressure of the take-off from Terra, beat through Raf's veins away from his laboring heart. He was helpless in the dark!

"Not alone—" the words came out of somewhere, he didn't know whether he heard them, or, in some queer way, felt them. "You are safe—not alone."

That brought a measure of comfort. But he was still in the dark, and he was moving—he could not will his hands to move—yet he was moving. He was being carried!

The flitter—he was back on the flitter! They were air-borne. But who was piloting?

"Captain! Soriki!" he appealed for reassurance. And then was aware that there was no familiar motor hum, none of that pressure of rushing air to which he had been so long accustomed that he missed it only now.

"You are safe—" Again that would-be comfort. But Raf tried to move his arms, twist his body, be sure that he rested in the flitter. Then another thought, only vaguely alarming at first, but which grew swiftly to panic proportions—He was in the alien globe—He was a prisoner!

"You are safe!" the words beat in his mind.

"But where—where?" he felt as if he were screaming that at the full power of his lungs. He must get out of this dark envelope, be free. Free! Free Men—He was Raf Kurbi of the Federation of Free Men, member of the crew of the Spacer *RS 10*. But there had been something else about free men—

Painfully he pulled fragments of pictures out of the past, assembled a jigsaw of wild action. And all of it ended in a blinding flash, blinding!

Raf cowered mentally if not physically, as his mind seized upon that last word. The blinding flash, then this depth of darkness. Had he been—?

"You are safe."

Maybe he was safe, he thought, with an anger born of honest fear, but was he—blind? And where was he? What had happened to him since that moment when the blast bomb had exploded?

"I am blind," he spat out, wanting to be told that his fears were only fears and not the truth.

"Your eyes are covered," the answer came quickly enough, and for a short space he was comforted until he realized that the reply was not a flat denial of his statement.

"Soriki?" he tried again. "Captain? Lablet?"

"Your companions"—there was a moment of hesitation, and then came what he was sure was the truth—"have escaped. Their ship took to the air when the Center was invaded."

So, he wasn't on the flitter. That was Raf's first reaction. Then, he must still be with the mermen, with the young stranger who claimed to be one of a lost Terran colony. But they couldn't leave him behind! Raf struggled against the power which held him motionless.

"Be quiet!" That was not soothing; it had the snap of a command, so sharp and with such authority in it that he obeyed. "You have been hurt; the gel must do its work. Sleep now. It is good to sleep—"

Dalgard walked by the hammock, using all the quieting power he possessed to ease the stranger, who now bore little resemblance to the lithe, swiftly moving, other-worldly figure of the day before. Stripped of his burned rags of clothing, coated with the healing stuff of the merpeople— that thick jelly substance which was their bulwark against illness and hurt—lashed into a hammock of sea fibers, he had the outward appearance of a thick bundle of supplies. The scout had seen miracles of healing performed by the gel, he could only hope for one now. "Sleep—" he made the soothing suggestion over and over and felt the other begin to relax, to sink into the semicoma in which he must rest for at least another day.

It was true that they had watched the strange flying machine take off from a roof top. And none of the mermen who had survived the battle which had raged through the city had seen any of the off-worlder's kind among the living or the dead of the alien forces. Perhaps, thinking Raf dead, they had returned to their space ship.

Now there were other, more immediate, problems to be met. They had done everything that they could to insure the well-being of the stranger, without whom they could not have delivered that one necessary blow which meant a new future for Astra.

The aliens were not all dead. Some had gone down under the spears of the mermen, but more of the sea people had died by the superior weapons of their foes. To the aliens, until they discovered what had happened to the globe and its cargo, it would seem an overwhelming triumph, for less than a quarter of the invading force fought its way back to safety in the underground ways. Yes, it would appear to be a victory for Those Others. But—now time was on the other side of the scales.

Dalgard doubted if the globe would ever fly again. And the loss of the storehouse plunder could never be repaired. By its destruction they had insured the future for their people, the mermen, the slowly growing settlement at Homeport.

They were well out of the city, in the open country, traveling along a rocky gorge, through which a river provided a highway to the sea. Dalgard had no idea as yet how he could win back across the waste of water to his own people. While the mermen with whom he had stormed the city were friendly, they were not of the tribes he knew, and their own connection with the eastern continent was through messages passed between islands and the depths.

Then there was the stranger—Dalgard knew that the ship which had brought him to this planet was somewhere in the north. Perhaps when he recovered, they could travel in that direction. But for the moment it was good just to be free, to feel the soft winds of summer lick his skin, to walk slowly under the sun, carrying the little bundle of things which belonged to the stranger, with a knife once more at his belt and friends about him.

But within the quarter-hour their peace was broken. Dalgard heard it first, his landsman's ears serving him where the complicated sense which gave the sea people warning did not operate. That shrill keening—he knew it of old. And at his warning the majority of the mermen plunged into the stream, becoming drifting shadows below the surface of the water. Only the four who were carrying the hammock stood their ground. But the scout, having told them to deposit their burden under the shelter of an overhanging ledge of rock, waved them to join their fellows. Until that menace in the sky was beaten, they dare not travel overland.

Was it still after him alone, hunting him by some mysterious built-in sense as it had overseas? He could see it now, moving in circles back and forth across the gorge, probably ready to dive on any prey venturing into the open.

Had it not been for the stranger, Dalgard could have taken to the water almost as quickly and easily as his companions. But they could not float the pilot down the stream, thus dissolving the thick coating of gel which was healing his terrible flash burns. And Those Others, were they following the trail of their mechanical hound as they had before?

Dalgard sent out questing tendrils of thought. Nowhere did he encounter the flashes which announced the proximity of Those Others. No, it would appear that they had unleashed the hound to do what damage it could, perhaps to serve them as a marker for a future counterattack. At present it was alone. And he relayed that information to the mermen.

If they could knock out the hound—his hand went to the tender scrape on his own scalp where that box had left its glancing mark—if they could knock out the hound—But how? As accurate marksmen as the mermen were with their spears, he was not sure they could bring down the box. Its sudden darts and dips were too erratic. Then what? Because as long as it bobbed there, he and the stranger were imprisoned in this pocket of the gorge wall.

Dalgard sat down, the bundle of the stranger's belongings beside him. Then, he carefully unfastened the scorched cloth which formed that bag and examined its contents. There was the belt with its pouches, sheaths, and tool case. And the weapon which the stranger had used to such good effect during their escape from the arena. Dalgard took up the gun. It was light in weight, and it fitted into his hand almost as if it had been molded to his measure.

He aimed at the hovering box, pressed the button as he had seen the other do, with no results. The stun ray, which had acted upon living creatures, could not govern the delicate mechanism in the hound's interior. Dalgard laid it aside. There were no more of the bombs, nor would they have been effective against such a target. As far as he could see, there was nothing among Raf's possessions which could help them now.

One of the black shadows in the water moved to shore. The box swooped, death striking at the merman who ran to shelter. A second followed him, eluding the attack of the hound by a matter of inches. Now the box buzzed angrily.

Dalgard, catching their thoughts, hurried to aid them. They undid the knots of the hammock about the helpless stranger, leaving about him only the necessary bandage ties. Now they had a crude net, woven, as Dalgard knew, of undersea fibers strong enough to hold captive plunging monsters a dozen times the size of the box. If they could net it!

He had seen the exploits of the mermen hunters, knew their skill with net and spear. But to scoop a flying thing out of the air was a new problem.

"Not so!" the thought cut across his. "They have used such as this to hunt us before, long ago. We had believed they were all lost. It must be caught and broken, or it will hunt and kill and hunt again, for it does not tire nor can it be beaten from any trail it is set upon. Now—"

"I will do that, for you have the knowledge—" the scout cut in quickly. After his other meeting with the hound he had no liking for the task he had taken on, but there must be bait to draw the box within striking distance.

"Stand upright and move toward those rocks." The mermen changed position, the net, now with stones in certain loops to weigh it, caught in their three-fingered hands.

Dalgard moved, fighting against hunching his shoulders, against hurrying the pace. He saw the shadow of the flitting death, and flung himself down beside the boulder the mermen had pointed out. Then he rolled over, half surprised not to be struck.

The hound was still in the air but over it now was draped the net, the rocks in its fringes weighing it down in spite of its jerky attempts to rise. In its struggles to be free, it might almost have led the watcher to believe that it had intelligence of a sort. Now the mermen were coming out of the stream, picking up rocks as they advanced. And a hail of stones flew through the air, while others of the sea people sprang to catch the dangling ends of the net and drag the captive to earth.

In the end they smashed it completely, burying the remains under a pile of rocks. Then, retrieving their net, they once more fastened Raf into it and turned downstream, as intent as ever upon reaching the sea. Dalgard wondered whether Those Others would ever discover what had become of their hound. Or had it in some way communicated with its masters, so that now they were aware that it had been destroyed. But he was sure they had nothing more to fear, that the way to the sea was open.

In mid-morning of the second day they came out upon shelving sand and saw before them the waves which promised safety and escape to the mermen. Dalgard sat down in the blue-gray sand beside Raf. The sea people had assured him that the stranger was making a good recovery, that within a matter of hours he could be freed from his cocoon of healing.

Dalgard squinted at the sun sparkling on the waves. Where now? To the north where the space ship waited? If what he read in Raf's mind was true the other wanted to leave Astra, to voyage back to that other world which was only a legend to Dalgard, and a black, unhappy legend at that. If the Elders were here, had a chance to contact these men from Terra— Dalgard's eyes narrowed, would they choose to? Another chain of thought had been slowly developing in his mind during these past hours when he had been so closely companioned with the stranger. And almost he had come to a decision which would have seemed very odd even days before.

No, there was no way of suddenly bringing the Elders here, of transferring his burden of decision to them. Dalgard cupped his chin in his hand and tried to imagine what it would be like to shut oneself up in a small metal-walled spacer and set out blindly to leave one world for another. His ancestors had done that, and they had traveled in cold sleep, ignorant of whether they would ever reach their goal. They had been very brave, or very desperate, men.

But—Dalgard measured sand, sun, and sky, watching the mermen sporting in the waves—but for him Astra was enough. He wanted nothing but this land, this world. There was nothing which drew him back. He would try to locate the spacer for the sake of the stranger; Astra owed Raf all they could manage to give him. But the ship was as alien to Homeport as it now existed as the city's globe might have been.

18

NOT YET—

Raf lay on his back, cushioned in the sand, his face turned up to the sky. Moisture smarted in his eyes, trickled down his cheeks as he tried to will himself to *see*! The yellow haze which had been his day had faded into grayness and now to the dark he feared so much that he dared not even speak of it. Somewhere over him the stars were icy points of light—but he could not see them. They were very far away, but no farther than he was from safety, from comfort (now the spacer seemed a haven of ease), from the expert treatment which might save, save his sight!

He supposed he should be thankful to that other one who was a slow voice speaking out of the mist, a thought now and then when his inner panic brought him almost to the breaking point. In some manner he had been carried out of the reach of the aliens, treated for his searing wounds, and now he was led along, fed, tended—Why didn't they go away and leave him alone! He had no chance of reaching the spacer—

It was so easy to remember those mountains, the heights over which he had lifted the flitter. There wasn't one chance in a million of his winning over those and across the miles of empty plains beyond to where the *RS 10* stood waiting, ready to rise again. The crew must believe him dead. His fists clenched upon sand, and it gritted between his fingers, sifted away. Why wasn't he dead! Why had that barbarian dragged him here, continued to coax him, put food into his hands, those hands which were only vague shapes when he held them just before his straining, aching eyes.

"It is not as bad as you think," the words came again out of the fog, spoken with a gentleness which rasped Raf's nerves. "Healing is not done in a second, or even in a day. You cannot force the return of strength—"

A hand, warm, vibrant with life, pressed on his forehead—a human, flesh-covered hand, not one of the cool, scaled paws of the furred people. Though those hands, too, had been laid upon him enough during the past few days, steadying him, leading him, guiding him to food and water. Now, under that firm, knowing touch he felt some of the ever-present fear subside, felt a relaxation.

"My ship—They will take off without me!" He could not help but voice that plaint, as he had so many times before during that foggy, nightmare journey.

"They have not done so yet."

He struggled up, flung off that calming hand, turned angrily toward where he thought the other was. "How can you be sure?"

"Word has come. The ship is still there, though the small flyer has returned to it."

This assurance was something new. Raf's suspicions could not stand up against the note of certainty in the other's voice. He got awkwardly to his feet. If the ship was still here, then they must still think him alive—They might come back! He had a chance—a real chance!

"Then they are waiting for me—They'll come!"

He could not see the soberness with which Dalgard listened to that. The star ship had not lifted, that message had found its way south, passed along by hopper and merman. But the scout doubted if the explorers were waiting for the return of Raf. He believed that they would not have left the city had they not thought the pilot already dead.

As to going north now—His picture of the land ahead had been built up from reports gained from the sea people. It could be done, but with Raf to be nursed and guided, lacking even the outrigger Dalgard had used in home waters, it would take days—weeks, probably—to cover the territory which lay between them and the plains where the star ship had planeted.

But he owed Raf a great deal, and it was summer, the season of warm calms. So far he had not been able to work out any plan for a return to his own land. It might be that they were both doomed to exile. But it was not necessary to face that drear future yet, not until they had expended every possible effort. So now he said willingly enough, "We are going north."

Raf sat down again in the sand. He wanted to run, to push on until his feet were too tired to carry him any farther. But now he fought that impulse, lay down once more. Though he doubted if he could sleep.

Dalgard watched the stars, sketched out a map of action for the morning. They must follow the shore line where they could keep in touch with the mermen, though along this coast the sea people did not come to land with the freedom their fellows showed on the eastern continent—they had lived too long in fear of Those Others.

But since the war party had reached the coast, there had been no sign of any retaliation, and as several days passed, Dalgard had begun to believe that they had little to fear. Perhaps the blow they had struck at the heart of the citadel had been more drastic than they had hoped. He had listened since that hour in the gorge for the shrilling of one of the air hounds. And when it did not come the thought that maybe it was the last of its kind had been heartening.

At last the scout lay down beside the off-world man, listening to the soft hiss of waves on sand, the distant cluttering of night insects. And his last waking thought was a wish for his bow.

There was another day of patient plodding; two, three. Raf, led by the hand, helped over rocks and obstacles which were only dark blurs to his watering eyes, raged inwardly and sometimes outwardly, against the slowness of their advance, his own helplessness. His fear grew until he refused to credit the fact that the blurs were sharpening in outline, that he could now count five fingers on the hand he sometimes waved despairingly before his face.

When he spoke of the future, he never said "if we reach the ship" but always "when," refusing to admit that perhaps they would not be in time. And Dalgard by his anxiety, tried to get more news from the north.

"When we get there, will you come back to earth with us?" the pilot asked suddenly on the fifth day.

It was a question Dalgard had once asked himself. But now

he knew the answer; there was only one he dared give.

"We are not ready—"

"I don't understand what you mean." Raf was almost querulous. "It is your home world. Pax is gone; the Federation would welcome you eagerly. Just think what it would mean—a Terran colony among the stars!"

"A Terran colony." Dalgard put out a hand, steadied Raf over a stretch of rough shingle. "Yes, once we were a Terran colony. But—can you now truthfully swear that I am a Terran like yourself?"

Raf faced the misty figure, trying to force his memory to put features there, to sharpen outlines. The scout was of middle height, a little shorter in stature than the crewmen with whom the pilot had lived so long. His hair was fair, as was his skin under its sun tan. He was unusually light on his feet and possessed a wiry strength Raf could testify to. But there was that disconcerting habit of mind reading and other elusive differences.

Dalgard smiled, though the other could not see that.

"You see," deliberately he used the mind touch as if to accent those differences the more, "once our roots were the same, but now from these roots different plants have grown. And we must be left to ourselves a space before we mingle once more. My father's father's father's father was a Terran, but I am—what? We have something that you have not, just as you have developed during centuries of separation qualities of mind and body we do not know. You live with machines. And, since we could not keep machines in this world, having no power to repair or rebuild, we have been forced to turn in other directions. To go back to the old ways now would be throwing away clues to mysteries we have not yet fully explored, turning aside from discoveries ready to be made. To you I am a barbarian, hardly higher in the scale of civilization than the mermen—"

Raf flushed, would have given a quick and polite denial, had he not known that his thoughts had been read. Dalgard laughed. His amusement was not directed against the pilot, rather it invited him to share the joke. And reluctantly, Raf's peeling lips relaxed in a smile.

"But," he offered one argument the other had not cited, "what if you do go down this other path of yours so far that we no longer have any common meeting ground?" He had forgotten his own problem in the other's.

"I do not believe that will ever happen. Perhaps our bodies may change; climate, food, ways of life can all influence the body. Our minds may change; already my people with each new generation are better equipped to use the mind touch, can communicate more clearly with the animals and the mermen. But those who were in the beginning born of Terra shall always have a common heritage. There are and will be other lost colonies among the stars. We could not have been the only outlaws who broke forth during the rule of Pax, and before the blight of that dictatorship, there were at least two expeditions that went forth on Galactic explorations.

"A thousand years from now stranger will meet with stranger, but when they make the sign of peace and sit down with one another, they shall find that words come more easily, though one may seem outwardly monstrous to the other. Only, *now* we must go our own way. We are youths setting forth on our journey of testing, while the Elders wish us well but stand aside."

"You don't want what we have to offer?" This was a new idea to Raf.

"Did you truly want what the city people had to offer?"

That caught the pilot up. He could remember with unusual distinctness how he had disliked, somehow feared the things they had brought from the city storehouse, how he had privately hoped that Hobart and Lablet would be content to let well enough alone and not bring that knowledge of an alien race back with them. If he had not secretly known that aversion, he would not have been able to destroy the globe and the treasures piled about it.

"But"—his protest was hot, angry—"we are not *them*! We can do much for you."

"Can you?" The calm question sank into his mind as might a stone into a troubled pool, and the ripples of its passing changed an idea or two. "I wish that you might see Homeport. Perhaps then it would be easier for you to understand. No, your knowledge is not corrupt, it would not carry with it the same seeds of disaster as that of Those Others. But it would be too easy for us to accept, to walk a softer road, to forget what we have so far won. Just give us time—"

Raf cupped his palms over his watering eyes. He wanted badly to see clearly the other's face, to be able to read his expression. Yet it seemed that somehow he *was* able to see that sober face, as sincere as the words in his mind.

"You will come again," Dalgard said with certainty. "And we shall be waiting because you, Raf Kurbi, made it possible." There was something so solemn about that that Raf looked up in surprise.

"When you destroyed the core of Those Other's holding, you gave us our chance. For had you not done that we, the mermen, the other harmless, happy creatures of this world, would have been wiped out. There would be no new beginning here, only a dark and horrible end."

Raf blinked; to his surprise that other figure standing in the direct sunlight did not waver, and beyond the proudly held head was a stretch of turquoise sky. He could see the color!

"Yes, you shall see with your eyes—and with your mind," now Dalgard spoke aloud. "And if the Spirit which rules all space is kind, you shall return to your own people. For you have served His cause well."

Then, as if he were embarrassed by his own solemnity, Dalgard ended with a most prosaic inquiry: "Would you like shellfish for eating?"

Moments later, wading out into the water-swirled sand, his boots kicked off, his toes feeling for the elusive shelled creatures no one could see, Raf felt happier, freer than he could ever remember having been before. It was going to be all right. He could *see*! He would find the ship! He laughed aloud at nothing and heard an answering chuckle and then a whoop of triumph from the scout stooping to claw one of their prey out of hiding.

It was after they had eaten that Dalgard asked another question, one which did not seem important to Raf. "You have a close friend among the crew of your ship?"

Raf hesitated. Now that he was obliged to consider the point, did he have any friends—let alone a close one—among the crew of the *RS 10*? Certainly he did not claim Wonstead who had shared his quarters—he honestly did not care if he never saw him again. The officers, the experts such as Lablet— quickly face and character of each swept through his mind and was as swiftly discarded. There was Soriki—He could not claim the com-tech as any special friend, but at least during their period together among the aliens he had come to know him better.

Now, as if Dalgard had read his mind—and he probably had, thought Raf with a flash of the old resentment—he had another question.

"And what was he—is he like?"

Though the pilot could see little reason for this he answered as best he could, trying to build first a physical picture of the com-tech and then doing a little guessing as to what lay under the other's space-burned skin.

Dalgard lay on his back, gazing up into the blue-green sky. Yet Raf knew that he was intent on every word. A merman padded up, settled down cross-legged beside the scout, as if he too were enthralled by the pilot's halting description of a man he might never see again. Then a second of the sea people came and a third, until Raf felt that some sort of a noiseless council was in progress. His words trailed away, and then Dalgard offered an explanation.

"It will take us many, many days to reach the place where your ship is. And before we are able to complete that journey your friends may be gone. So we shall try something else— with your aid."

Raf fingered the little bundle of his possessions. Even his helmet with its com phone was missing.

"No," again Dalgard read his mind. "Your machines are of

no use to you now. We shall try *our* way."

"How?" Wild thoughts of a big signal fire—But how could that be sighted across a mountain range. Of some sort of an improvised com unit—

"I said *our* way." There was a smile on Dalgard's face, visible to Raf's slowly clearing vision. "We shall provide another kind of machine, and these"—he waved at the mermen—"will give us the power, or so we hope. Lie here," he gestured to the sand beside him, "and think only of your friend in the ship, in his natural surroundings. Try to hold that picture constant in your mind, letting no other thought trouble it."

"Do you mean—send a message to him mentally!" Raf's reply was half protest.

"Did I not so reach you when we were in the city—even before I knew of you as an individual?" the scout reminded him. "And such messages are doubly possible when they are sent from friend to friend."

"But we were close then."

"That is why—" again Dalgard indicated the mermen. "For them this is the natural means of communication. They will pick up your reaching thought, amplify it with their power, beam it north. Since your friend deals with matters of communication, let us hope that he will be sensitive to this method."

Raf was only half convinced that it might work But he remembered how Dalgard had established contact with him, before, as the scout had pointed out, they had met. It was that voiceless cry for aid which had pulled him into this adventure in the first place. It was only fitting that something of the same process give *him* help in return.

Obediently he stretched out on the sand and closed his dim eyes, trying to picture Soriki in the small cabin which held the com, slouched in his bucket seat, his deceptive posture that of a lax idler, as he had seen him so many times. Soriki—his broad face with its flat cheekbones, its wide cheerful mouth, its heavy-lidded eyes. And having fixed Soriki's face, he tried to believe that he was now confronting the com-tech, speaking directly to him.

"Come—come and get me—south—seashore—Soriki come and get me!" The words formed a kind of chant, a chant aimed at that familiar face in its familiar surroundings. "South—come and get me—" Raf struggled to think only of that, to allow nothing to break through that chant or disturb his picture of the scene he had called from memory.

How long that attempt at communication lasted the pilot could not tell, for somehow he slipped from the deep concentration into sleep, dreamless and untroubled, from which he awoke with the befogged feeling that something important had happened. But had he gotten through?

The ring of mermen was gone, and it was dawn, gray, chill with the forewarnings of rain in the air. He was reassured because he was certain that in spite of the gloom his sight was a fraction clearer than it had been the day before. But had they gotten through? As he arose, brushing the sand from him, he saw the scout splashing out of the sea, a fish impaled on his spear.

"Did we get through?" Raf blurted out.

"Since your friend cannot reply with the mind touch, we do

not know. But later we shall try again." To Raf's peering gaze Dalgard's face had a drawn, gaunt look as if he had been at hard labor during the hours just past. He walked up the beach slowly, without the springing step Raf had come to associate with him. As he settled down to gut the fish with one of the bone knives, the scout repeated, "We can try again—!"

Half an hour later, as the rain swept in from the sea, Raf knew that they would not have to try. His head went up, his face eager. He had known that sound too long and too well ever to mistake it—the drone of a flitter motor cutting through the swish of the falling water. Some trick of the cliffs behind them must be magnifying and projecting the sound, for he could not sight the machine. But it was coming. He whirled to Dalgard, only to see that the other was on his feet and had taken up his spear.

"It is the flitter! Soriki heard—they're coming!" Raf hastened to assure him.

For the last time he saw Dalgard's slow, warm smile, clearer than he had ever seen it before. Then the scout turned and trotted away, toward a fringing rock wall. Before he dropped out of sight behind that barrier he raised the spear in salute.

"Swift and fortunate voyaging!" He gave the farewell of Homeport.

Then Raf understood. The colonist meant just what he had said: he wanted no contact with the space ship. To Raf he had owed a debt and now that was paid. But the time was not yet when the men of Astra and the men of Terra should meet. A hundred years from now perhaps—or a thousand—but not yet. And remembering what had summoned the flitter winging toward him, Raf drew a deep breath. What would the men of Astra accomplish in a hundred years? What could those of Terra do to match them in knowledge? It was a challenge, and he alone knew just how much of a challenge. Homeport must remain his own secret. He had been guided to this place, saved by the mermen alone. Dalgard and his people must not exist as far as the crew of the *RS 10* were concerned.

For the last time he experienced the intimacy of the mind touch. "That is it—brother!" Then the sensation was gone as the black blot of the flitter buzzed out of the clouds.

From behind the rocks Dalgard watched the pilot enter the strange machine. For a single moment he had an impulse to shout, to run forward, to surrender to his desire to see the others, the ship which had brought them through space and would, they confidently believed, take them back to the Terra he knew only as a legend of the past. But he mastered that desire. He had been right. The road had already forked and there was no going back. He must carry this secret all the rest of his life—he must be strong-willed enough so that Homeport would never know. Time—give them time to be what they could be. Then in a hundred years—or a thousand—But not yet!

* * * * *

"Nobody today is telling better stories of straight-forward interstellar adventure."

—*New York Herald-Tribune*

When Raf Kurbi's Terran spaceship burst into unexplored skies of the far planet Astra and was immediately made welcome by the natives of a once-mighty metropolis, Kurbi was unaware of three vital things:

One was that Astra already harbored an Earth colony—descended from refugees from the world of the previous century.

Two was that these men and women were facing the greatest danger of their existence from a new outburst of the inhuman fiends who had once tyrannized Astra.

Three was that the natives who were buying Kurbi's science know-how were those very fiends—and their intentions were implacably deadly for all humans, whether Earth born or STAR BORN.

It's an Andre Norton space adventure—and therefore the tops in its field!

* * * * *

ABOUT THE AUTHOR

Andre Alice Norton (February 17, 1912 – March 17, 2005), science fiction and fantasy author (with some works of historical fiction and contemporary fiction), was born Alice Mary Norton in Cleveland, Ohio, in the United States. She published her first novel in 1934. She was the first woman to receive the Gandalf Grand Master Award from the World Science Fiction Society in 1977, and she won the Damon Knight Memorial Grand Master Award from the SFWA in 1983. She wrote under the noms de plume Andre Norton, Andrew North and Allen Weston.

After graduating from high school in 1930, Norton continued her education at Flora Stone Mather College of Western Reserve University. In 1932, she began working for the Cleveland Library System and remained there for 18 years, latterly in the children's section of the Nottingham Branch Library in Cleveland. She legally changed her name to Andre Alice Norton in 1934 to appeal to a predominantly male audience and to increase her marketability. From 1940 to 1941, she worked as a special librarian in the cataloguing department of the Library of Congress, involved in a project related to alien citizenship. The project was abruptly terminated upon American entry into World War II.

In most Norton books, whether SF or fantasy, the plot takes place in the open countryside, with only short episodes in a city environment.

Choose from Thousands of 1stWorldLibrary Classics By

A. M. Barnard
Ada Leverson
Adolphus William Ward
Aesop
Agatha Christie
Alexander Aaronsohn
Alexander Kielland
Alexandre Dumas
Alfred Gatty
Alfred Ollivant
Alice Duer Miller
Alice Turner Curtis
Alice Dunbar
Allen Chapman
Alleyne Ireland
Ambrose Bierce
Amelia E. Barr
Amory H. Bradford
Andrew Lang
Andrew McFarland Davis
Andy Adams
Angela Brazil
Anna Alice Chapin
Anna Sewell
Annie Besant
Annie Hamilton Donnell
Annie Payson Call
Annie Roe Carr
Annonaymous
Anton Chekhov
Archibald Lee Fletcher
Arnold Bennett
Arthur C. Benson
Arthur Conan Doyle
Arthur M. Winfield
Arthur Ransome
Arthur Schnitzler
Arthur Train
Atticus
B.H. Baden-Powell
B. M. Bower
B. C. Chatterjee
Baroness Emmuska Orczy
Baroness Orczy
Basil King
Bayard Taylor
Ben Macomber
Bertha Muzzy Bower
Bjornstjerne Bjornson

Booth Tarkington
Boyd Cable
Bram Stoker
C. Collodi
C. E. Orr
C. M. Ingleby
Carolyn Wells
Catherine Parr Traill
Charles A. Eastman
Charles Amory Beach
Charles Dickens
Charles Dudley Warner
Charles Farrar Browne
Charles Ives
Charles Kingsley
Charles Klein
Charles Hanson Towne
Charles Lathrop Pack
Charles Romyn Dake
Charles Whibley
Charles Willing Beale
Charlotte M. Braeme
Charlotte M. Yonge
Charlotte Perkins Stetson
Clair W. Hayes
Clarence Day Jr.
Clarence E. Mulford
Clemence Housman
Confucius
Coningsby Dawson
Cornelis DeWitt Wilcox
Cyril Burleigh
D. H. Lawrence
Daniel Defoe
David Garnett
Dinah Craik
Don Carlos Janes
Donald Keyhoe
Dorothy Kilner
Dougan Clark
Douglas Fairbanks
E. Nesbit
E. P. Roe
E. Phillips Oppenheim
E. S. Brooks
Earl Barnes
Edgar Rice Burroughs
Edith Van Dyne
Edith Wharton

Edward Everett Hale
Edward J. O'Biren
Edward S. Ellis
Edwin L. Arnold
Eleanor Atkins
Eleanor Hallowell Abbott
Eliot Gregory
Elizabeth Gaskell
Elizabeth McCracken
Elizabeth Von Arnim
Ellem Key
Emerson Hough
Emilie F. Carlen
Emily Bronte
Emily Dickinson
Enid Bagnold
Enilor Macartney Lane
Erasmus W. Jones
Ernie Howard Pie
Ethel May Dell
Ethel Turner
Ethel Watts Mumford
Eugene Sue
Eugenie Foa
Eugene Wood
Eustace Hale Ball
Evelyn Everett-green
Everard Cotes
F. H. Cheley
F. J. Cross
F. Marion Crawford
Fannie E. Newberry
Federick Austin Ogg
Ferdinand Ossendowski
Fergus Hume
Florence A. Kilpatrick
Fremont B. Deering
Francis Bacon
Francis Darwin
Frances Hodgson Burnett
Frances Parkinson Keyes
Frank Gee Patchin
Frank Harris
Frank Jewett Mather
Frank L. Packard
Frank V. Webster
Frederic Stewart Isham
Frederick Trevor Hill
Frederick Winslow Taylor

Friedrich Kerst
Friedrich Nietzsche
Fyodor Dostoyevsky
G.A. Henty
G.K. Chesterton
Gabrielle E. Jackson
Garrett P. Serviss
Gaston Leroux
George A. Warren
George Ade
Geroge Bernard Shaw
George Cary Eggleston
George Durston
George Ebers
George Eliot
George Gissing
George MacDonald
George Meredith
George Orwell
George Sylvester Viereck
George Tucker
George W. Cable
George Wharton James
Gertrude Atherton
Gordon Casserly
Grace E. King
Grace Gallatin
Grace Greenwood
Grant Allen
Guillermo A. Sherwell
Gulielma Zollinger
Gustav Flaubert
H. A. Cody
H. B. Irving
H.C. Bailey
H. G. Wells
H. H. Munro
H. Irving Hancock
H. R. Naylor
H. Rider Haggard
H. W. C. Davis
Haldeman Julius
Hall Caine
Hamilton Wright Mabie
Hans Christian Andersen
Harold Avery
Harold McGrath
Harriet Beecher Stowe
Harry Castlemon
Harry Coghill
Harry Houidini

Hayden Carruth
Helent Hunt Jackson
Helen Nicolay
Hendrik Conscience
Hendy David Thoreau
Henri Barbusse
Henrik Ibsen
Henry Adams
Henry Ford
Henry Frost
Henry James
Henry Jones Ford
Henry Seton Merriman
Henry W Longfellow
Herbert A. Giles
Herbert Carter
Herbert N. Casson
Herman Hesse
Hildegard G. Frey
Homer
Honore De Balzac
Horace B. Day
Horace Walpole
Horatio Alger Jr.
Howard Pyle
Howard R. Garis
Hugh Lofting
Hugh Walpole
Humphry Ward
Ian Maclaren
Inez Haynes Gillmore
Irving Bacheller
Isabel Cecilia Williams
Isabel Hornibrook
Israel Abrahams
Ivan Turgenev
J.G.Austin
J. Henri Fabre
J. M. Barrie
J. M. Walsh
J. Macdonald Oxley
J. R. Miller
J. S. Fletcher
J. S. Knowles
J. Storer Clouston
J. W. Duffield
Jack London
Jacob Abbott
James Allen
James Andrews
James Baldwin

James Branch Cabell
James DeMille
James Joyce
James Lane Allen
James Lane Allen
James Oliver Curwood
James Oppenheim
James Otis
James R. Driscoll
Jane Abbott
Jane Austen
Jane L. Stewart
Janet Aldridge
Jens Peter Jacobsen
Jerome K. Jerome
Jessie Graham Flower
John Buchan
John Burroughs
John Cournos
John F. Kennedy
John Gay
John Glasworthy
John Habberton
John Joy Bell
John Kendrick Bangs
John Milton
John Philip Sousa
John Taintor Foote
Jonas Lauritz Idemil Lie
Jonathan Swift
Joseph A. Altsheler
Joseph Carey
Joseph Conrad
Joseph E. Badger Jr
Joseph Hergesheimer
Joseph Jacobs
Jules Vernes
Julian Hawthrone
Julie A Lippmann
Justin Huntly McCarthy
Kakuzo Okakura
Karle Wilson Baker
Kate Chopin
Kenneth Grahame
Kenneth McGaffey
Kate Langley Bosher
Kate Langley Bosher
Katherine Cecil Thurston
Katherine Stokes
L. A. Abbot
L. T. Meade

L. Frank Baum
Latta Griswold
Laura Dent Crane
Laura Lee Hope
Laurence Housman
Lawrence Beasley
Leo Tolstoy
Leonid Andreyev
Lewis Carroll
Lewis Sperry Chafer
Lilian Bell
Lloyd Osbourne
Louis Hughes
Louis Joseph Vance
Louis Tracy
Louisa May Alcott
Lucy Fitch Perkins
Lucy Maud Montgomery
Luther Benson
Lydia Miller Middleton
Lyndon Orr
M. Corvus
M. H. Adams
Margaret E. Sangster
Margret Howth
Margaret Vandercook
Margaret W. Hungerford
Margret Penrose
Maria Edgeworth
Maria Thompson Daviess
Mariano Azuela
Marion Polk Angellotti
Mark Overton
Mark Twain
Mary Austin
Mary Catherine Crowley
Mary Cole
Mary Hastings Bradley
Mary Roberts Rinehart
Mary Rowlandson
M. Wollstonecraft Shelley
Maud Lindsay
Max Beerbohm
Myra Kelly
Nathaniel Hawthrone
Nicolo Machiavelli
O. F. Walton
Oscar Wilde

Owen Johnson
P.G. Wodehouse
Paul and Mabel Thorne
Paul G. Tomlinson
Paul Severing
Percy Brebner
Percy Keese Fitzhugh
Peter B. Kyne
Plato
Quincy Allen
R. Derby Holmes
R. L. Stevenson
R. S. Ball
Rabindranath Tagore
Rahul Alvares
Ralph Bonehill
Ralph Henry Barbour
Ralph Victor
Ralph Waldo Emmerson
Rene Descartes
Ray Cummings
Rex Beach
Rex E. Beach
Richard Harding Davis
Richard Jefferies
Richard Le Gallienne
Robert Barr
Robert Frost
Robert Gordon Anderson
Robert L. Drake
Robert Lansing
Robert Lynd
Robert Michael Ballantyne
Robert W. Chambers
Rosa Nouchette Carey
Rudyard Kipling
Saint Augustine
Samuel B. Allison
Samuel Hopkins Adams
Sarah Bernhardt
Sarah C. Hallowell
Selma Lagerlof
Sherwood Anderson
Sigmund Freud
Standish O'Grady
Stanley Weyman
Stella Benson
Stella M. Francis

Stephen Crane
Stewart Edward White
Stijn Streuvels
Swami Abhedananda
Swami Parmananda
T. S. Ackland
T. S. Arthur
The Princess Der Ling
Thomas A. Janvier
Thomas A Kempis
Thomas Anderton
Thomas Bailey Aldrich
Thomas Bulfinch
Thomas De Quincey
Thomas Dixon
Thomas H. Huxley
Thomas Hardy
Thomas More
Thornton W. Burgess
U. S. Grant
Upton Sinclair
Valentine Williams
Various Authors
Vaughan Kester
Victor Appleton
Victor G. Durham
Victoria Cross
Virginia Woolf
Wadsworth Camp
Walter Camp
Walter Scott
Washington Irving
Wilbur Lawton
Wilkie Collins
Willa Cather
Willard F. Baker
William Dean Howells
William le Queux
W. Makepeace Thackeray
William W. Walter
William Shakespeare
Winston Churchill
Yei Theodora Ozaki
Yogi Ramacharaka
Young E. Allison
Zane Grey

Printed in the United States
96728LV00003B/54/A

9 781421 846934